NUMBER EIGHTEEN:

The Walter Prescott Webb Memorial Lectures

Essays on the Postbellum Southern Economy

[THE WALTER PRESCOTT WEBB MEMORIAL LECTURES]

Essays on the Postbellum Southern Economy

BY THAVOLIA GLYMPH, HAROLD D. WOODMAN,

BARBARA JEANNE FIELDS,

ARMSTEAD L. ROBINSON

Introduction by THAVOLIA GLYMPH
Edited by THAVOLIA GLYMPH
and JOHN J. KUSHMA

Published for the University of Texas at Arlington by
Texas A&M University Press: College Station

Library of Congress Cataloging in Publication Data
Main entry under title:

Essays on the postbellum southern economy.

(The Walter Prescott Webb memorial lectures ; 18)
Includes bibliographies.
1. Southern States—Economic conditions—Addresses,
essays, lectures.   I. Glymph, Thavolia, 1951–
II. Kushma, John J. (John James), 1949–
III. University of Texas at Arlington.   IV. Series.
HC107.A13E75   1985   330.975   84-40564
ISBN 0-89096-227-8

Manufactured in the United States of America
FIRST EDITION

Contents

Preface

THE eighteenth annual Walter Prescott Webb Memorial Lectures were presented on March 10, 1983, at the University of Texas at Arlington. The theme was the postbellum southern economy, with a particular focus on the transition to capitalist agriculture in areas previously dominated by chattel slavery. The subject of regional economic differences in the United States was a primary focus of Walter Prescott Webb's scholarship, one that he explored most fully in *Divided We Stand*. We are sure that he would have joined the large audience in finding these lectures both stimulating and edifying.

With the exception of the introduction by Thavolia Glymph, the essays in this volume were originally delivered as the eighteenth annual Webb Lectures. Barbara J. Fields, of the University of Michigan, Thavolia Glymph, of the University of Texas at Arlington, Armstead L. Robinson, of the University of Virginia, and Harold D. Woodman, of Purdue University, were the invited speakers whose lectures are reproduced in this volume.

On behalf of the Department of History of the University of Texas at Arlington, the editors would like to thank C. B. Smith, Sr., of Austin, Texas, a student and friend of Walter Webb, whose generosity in providing financial support has aided in the presentation of these lectures. We would also like to acknowledge our indebtedness to Jenkins Garrett, a friend and benefactor of the University of Texas at Arlington and the Department of History.

Sue Bailey, of the Freedmen and Southern Society Project, gave generously of her time in the preparation of this manuscript. We acknowledge her contributions.

THAVOLIA GLYMPH
JOHN J. KUSHMA

Essays on the Postbellum
Southern Economy

THAVOLIA GLYMPH

Introduction

IN 1866, an Alabama ex-slave, writing to the state's assistant commissioner of the Bureau of Refugees, Freedmen, and Abandoned Lands, described the plight of himself and other former slaves who were attempting to become independent farmers. They needed credit to obtain supplies to produce a cotton crop, Philip Smith explained, and local whites refused to assist. He appealed to the government for help to be repaid when their cotton was harvested. Impressing upon the bureau officer the urgency of their situation, as they no longer wished to work for whites, Smith asserted, "We are all free and Wish an onrable life."[1]

As Smith's statement affirmed, the former slaves believed that securing their freedom was incompatible with continuing to work for their former masters. By an honorable life they had in mind a specific kind of independence. It included land, freedom from white supervision, and freedom to control their lives and the disposition of their labor. Unlike Smith, however, the majority of the former slaves would not realize their fondest hope of land ownership. This they quickly discovered as the radical camp in the North retreated from the revolutionary step of land confiscation and redistribution and southern whites mobilized to ensure that even in the hour of their greatest tribulation land would not be made available to their former slaves. Yet though continuity in ownership of land prevailed, at least up to 1870, there was discontinuity in almost every other sphere of life. The essays in this volume attempt to analyze the circumstances that made the postwar South, in fundamental ways, the New South.

Central to the theses outlined in these essays is the revolutionary impact of emancipation. The slaves were now free men and women, and the masters were stripped of their customary access to power and affluence. That circumstance, these essays contend, was at once the bottom line and the top. Landless blacks would have to be transformed into agricultural wage workers and landed whites into employers of free labor before staple crop production could be revitalized. In the transformation of the American South, as in all post-emancipation societies, this task took precedence over all others. The economic reconstruction of the South remained the central problem long after political reconstruction had been established and then expunged.

The postbellum South has elicited and generated substantial comment from historians, and in recent years the work of scholars has not only increased quantitatively but widened to encompass areas and topics previously ignored. Greater attention to the problems attendant upon the reconstruction of lives and labor, both black and white, and to the impact of the different circumstances of slavery and emancipation has greatly enriched our understanding of the period.[2] The picture emerging is both far more complicated and much richer than was once imagined. It is now clear, for instance, that the reconstruction of the plantation South proceeded much differently in the lowcountry of South Carolina, where the freedpeople by the end of the war had de facto possession of both land and labor, than it did in the black belt of Mississippi, where former masters and northern planters held sway, at least in the matter of land, and differently still in the sugar cane fields of Louisiana, where the infusion of northern capital seems to have led to an almost immediate adoption of a wage labor system. It proceeded differently as well where the circumstances of slavery—such as the task system or absentee planters—had allowed room for the emergence of an independent black culture or the participation of slaves in local market economies and exchange relations. How and when freedom arrived was equally significant.

What the story of the postbellum South everywhere shares, however, is the forging of new social relationships which, whatever the residual elements from the past, were compelled by the North's military triumph and the concomitant commitment to freedom which it carried and validated in its wake. As Armstead Robinson maintains, "Both defeat and emancipation mattered." Thus, the essays that follow endeavor to place the transition to a free labor economy in the southern United States more firmly in its social and economic context, but not without regard to its political context.[3] Towards that end, they contribute, in part, to that literature which views the world-wide emancipations of the nineteenth century as events which, as Barbara J. Fields shows, decisively propelled the advent of capitalist agriculture, exemplified in the American South by the new plantation system whose development Harold D. Woodman analyzes. My own contribution attempts to trace the development of the share-wage system and its evolution into the institution of sharecropping that, in the end, reduced the former slaves to the position of wage workers, confirming the arrival of capitalist social relations.[4]

Armstead Robinson correctly insists in his essay that insight into the character of social change in the postbellum South must be rooted in studies of the collapse of slavery and the rise of new labor arrangements during the Civil War.[5] Focusing on three subregions of the Mississippi Valley—its upper South, southern Louisiana, and the cotton South—Robinson explores the dynamics between the particularities of slavery in each and the arrival of wartime freedom, showing how, in the end, freedom engulfed all; this despite President Abraham Lincoln's oft-repeated declaration of having no desire to interfere with the property rights of the southern rebels, and the determination of northern military officers to confine the terms of the war to the political question of Union. The actions of antislavery soldiers, inflated by conversions to the cause of freedom on the field of battle, defiance by short-handed military commanders of orders to turn away fugitive slaves, northern political activities favoring abolition, and the erosion of slavery in the loyal slave states all pointed in a direction different from that pronounced by Lincoln.[6]

Eventually, the federal government also came to understand, as Fields argues, that "there could be no ultimate compromise between the sovereignty of a bourgeois nation-state and the sovereignty of master over slave." In increasingly more forthright commitments—in the form of confiscation acts, an article of war, the Emancipation Proclamation, and, ultimately, a constitutional amendment—the federal government gradually but decisively shifted the meaning of the conflict to that which the slaves had articulated from the first. The slaves themselves had promoted that shift with each new accession to the ranks of the fugitive slave population and, perhaps most symbolically important, by enlisting as soldiers in the army that fought their masters.[7]

By the end of the war, black freedom had been gained in, as Robinson puts it, "small and painfully won increments." Still, each bitterly contested accretion undermined the sovereignty of master over slave, even in interior areas untouched directly by battles of war. Indeed, long before the collapse of the Confederacy's bid for nationhood, southern whites had become party to the demise of the world they had gone to war to preserve. Confederate impressment, refugeeing, and the breaking of ranks between non-slaveholding and slaveholding whites all contributed. If, however, as Robinson makes clear, the arrival of wartime freedom did not often signal the emergence of the particular kind of freedom blacks sought, as the title of his essay indicates, it nevertheless signaled the emergence of a new set of social relationships, constituting the primordial ground upon which the new order would have to be built. The outlines of the new contest were soon clear, and, as Thomas C. Holt has pointed out, in the American South, as in all post-emancipation societies, "defining freedom was the beginning of the difficulty."[8]

Even with freedom secured by constitutional amendments, the former slaves encountered resistance to their notions of what it ought to mean: the right of access to land; the right to sell their labor power and to fish and hunt as they chose; and the right to control the labor of their families. My own essay concerns the former slaves' attempts to secure this kind of freedom, in the absence of landownership, under the system of share wages prevalent between 1865 and 1867. Unlike some scholars who have chronicled their past, the former slaves came to understand quickly enough that the question of land was, for the moment, moot.[9] While land ownership, more than anything else, embodied their specific conception of freedom, it was the conception, in the end, that mattered. When denied land, their struggle to define labor relations continued to incorporate that conception of freedom. Their preference for share wages embodied that struggle.

To the freedpeople, their labor power was of no less consequence to the making of a crop than was the planters' land. It was, after all, their labor that gave value to the land. They therefore claimed, when working for a share of the crop, the right to participate in decisions that affected the making of the crop, not simply because these decisions affected the balance sheet at the end of the harvest, but also because they affected the content and meaning of freedom. Both their interpretation of labor relations and the world view of which it was a part clashed directly with the interests of their former masters. The freedpeople's view also countered northern notions of how the South was to be remade.

While northerners generally agreed that the former slaves had to be transformed into free workers, former masters into businessmen, and white yeomen into commercial farmers, their initial presumption as to how easily these transformations would be accomplished, Woodman stresses, proved unwarranted. Neither the former slaves nor their former masters behaved in the prescribed way once the fetters of slavery were removed, defying the central tenets of northern free labor ideology. Woodman argues that their behavior reflected, in part, the legacy of slavery, because emancipation had created the conditions for the establishment of a free labor system but neither the institutions nor the ideology necessary for its operation. The immediate result, therefore, was the emergence of a free labor system delimited, on the one hand, by a past experience now irrelevant and, on the other, by a free labor ideology itself fragmented and, in part, anachronistic.

Apart from some circumstances peculiar to the American South, the transformation of the South to a free labor economy, Woodman maintains, involved problems that were becoming increasingly familiar in the creation of an industrial working class, those of labor-management relations.[10] Yet, as Woodman stresses here and elsewhere, a general neglect by historians of the economic and social consequences of emancipation, an emphasis on the theme of continuity rather than examinations of the kind of change that took place, and a failure to apply the insights of labor historians who have studied the transformation of agricultural workers into an industrial working class, have combined to cloud analysis, in studies of the nineteenth-century South, of the social revolution accomplished by emancipation and the revolution not accomplished.[11]

Emancipation, Woodman concludes, was insufficient, in and of itself, to guarantee the triumph of a completely new order. However, by the end of the nineteenth century, capitalist social relations had spread through the southern backcountry and lowcountry (ensnaring the southern yeomanry as well as the former slaves and former masters). The majority of southern blacks had been transformed into wage hands, and a new business class, with a changed ideology and a changed relationship to the means of production, had arisen, even if the ideology of free labor that stressed new work rhythms and responsibilities had not thoroughly penetrated the ideology of either the workers or the planter businessmen. The southern way remained peculiar.

Erratic as was its path, the advance of capitalist relations in southern agriculture, Fields insists, was part and parcel of the advent and growing domination of bourgeois social relations on a world-wide scale, fed by what Eric Hobsbawm has denominated the "dual revolution."[12] That the spread of capitalist relations sometimes "engendered its own opposite," Fields contends, served only to delay rather than deter its advance. Her essay traces that erratic path, placing the southern context within a global framework, with particular attention to the role of the state, the balance of political power, and the collaboration of the slaves themselves in the process of emancipation and the establishment of new social and political relationships.

In the American South, planters eventually regained political power, but not before crucial decisions had been made in their absence and not before they had lost their old means of extracting the agricultural surplus. Furthermore, the triumph of capitalist social relations in southern agriculture was not, in all ways, a victory for the planter class. Sharecropping stood as an unambiguous defeat of the former slaves. But as Fields stresses, sharecropping became, as well, a symbol of the planters' defeat: their inability to come back fully on their own terms.

Thus, ironically, sharecropping became the emblem of the defeat of both the former slaves and their former masters and, simultaneously, the symbol of the triumph of capitalist social relations of a particular kind. In the end, the consequences were catastrophic for all southerners, but particularly for blacks. Blacks had lost their bid for independence. Few of the notions that had imbued their definition of freedom and their preference for share wages withstood the onslaught of the increasing dominance of capitalist social relations. If defining freedom had posed problems in the aftermath of war, the meaning of their "unfreedom" as sharecroppers was explicit.[13] They now had no rights in any decisions affecting the production of the crop, and by the end of the nineteenth century they were subjected to an intensification of economic, political, and social oppression. In significant ways their loss became that of the region's as a whole. The South itself remained the economic backwater of the new Union well into the twentieth century.

Notes

1. Phil Smith to freedmons buro [sic], April 5, 1866, Unregistered Letters Received, ser. 9, Alabama Assistant Commissioner, Records of the Bureau of Refugees, Freedmen, and Abandoned Lands (RG 105), National Archives (NA) [A–1777]. Bracketed letter groups, here and throughout, refer to file numbers of copies of documents from the National Archives that are housed at the Freedmen and Southern Society Project, University of Maryland, College Park.

2. Surveys of some of the recent literature and ongoing debate among scholars on key issues concerning this period may be found in Harold D. Woodman, "Sequel to Slavery: The New History Views the Postbellum South," *Journal of Southern History* 44 (Nov., 1977): 523–54; Eric Foner, "Reconstruction Revisited," *Reviews in American History* 10 (Dec., 1982): 82–100; Bernard A. Weisberger, "The Dark and Bloody Ground of Reconstruction Historiography," *Journal of Southern History* 25 (Nov., 1959): 427–47; Richard O. Curry, "The Civil War and Reconstruction, 1861–1877: A Critical Overview of Recent Trends and Interpretations," *Civil War History* 20 (Sept., 1974): 215–28; Gavin Wright, "The Strange Career of the New Southern Economic History," *Reviews in American History* 10 (Dec., 1982): 164–80. Important recent studies include: Barbara J. Fields, *Slavery and Freedom on the Middle Ground: Maryland during the Nineteenth Century* (New Haven: Yale Univ. Press, forthcoming); Eric Foner, *Nothing But Freedom: Emancipation and Its Legacy* (Baton Rouge: Louisiana State Univ. Press, 1983); Armstead Robinson, *Bitter Fruits of Bondage: Slavery's Demise and the Collapse of the Confederacy* (New Haven: Yale Univ. Press, 1985); Joseph P. Reidy, "The Development of Central Factories and the Rise of Tenancy in Louisiana's Sugar Economy, 1880–1910," (paper delivered at annual meeting of the Social Science History Association, Chicago, Ill., Nov., 1982); Joseph P. Reidy, "Masters and Slaves, Planters and Freedmen: The Transition from Slavery to Freedom in Central Georgia, 1820–1880," (Ph.D. diss., Northern Illinois Univ., 1982). The work of Steven Hahn forms an indispensable part of this literature, as it contributes to an understanding of the impact of the Civil War, reconstruction, and the establishment of capitalist agriculture in the postbellum South among white yeomen, suggesting important connections between the transformation of the yeoman economy and the subjugation of the former slaves. See "Common Right and Commonwealth: The Stock Law Struggle and the Roots of Southern Populism," in *Region, Race and Reconstruction: Essays in Honor of C. Vann Woodward*, ed. J. Morgan Kousser and James M. McPherson (New York: Oxford Univ. Press, 1982); "Hunting, Fishing, and Foraging and the Transformation of Property Rights in the Postbellum South," *Radical History Review* 26 (1982); and *The Roots of Southern Populism: Yeoman Farmers and the Transformation of the Georgia Upcountry, 1850–1890* (New York: Oxford Univ. Press, 1983). Leslie S. Rowland's unpublished material on the lowcountry rice plantations also promises to further an understanding of this period. Eugene D. Genovese's pathbreaking studies on American slavery have no doubt been of major significance in shifting the focus of studies of the postwar South. See *Roll Jordan Roll: The World the Slaves Made* (New York: Pantheon, 1974); *The Political Economy of Slavery: Studies in the Economy and Society of the New South* (New York: Pantheon, 1965); *The World the Slaveholders Made: Two Essays in Interpretation* (New York: Pantheon, 1969). C. Vann Woodward, *Origins of the New South* (Baton Rouge: Louisiana Univ. Press, 1951), remains an important standard.

3. In a comparative analysis of selected post-emancipation societies, Eric Foner

discusses more fully the American political context, with particular attention to the fundamental reordering necessitated by the granting of the elective franchise to freedmen. See *Nothing But Freedom*, 39–73 and *passim*.

4.   On this question see, for instance, Barrington Moore, Jr., *Social Origins of Dictatorship and Democracy: Lord and Peasant in the Making of the Modern World* (Boston: Beacon Press, 1966); E. J. Hobsbawm, *The Age of Capital, 1848–1875* (New York: Charles Scribners, 1975); E. J. Hobsbawm, *The Age of Revolution, 1789–1848* (New York: Charles Scribners, 1964); Rodney Hilton, *The Transition from Feudalism to Capitalism* (London: Unwin Brothers, 1976).

5.   The work of W. E. B. Du Bois remains an indispensable starting point. See especially *Black Reconstruction in America: An Essay Toward a History of the Part Which Black Folk Played in the Attempt to Reconstruct Democracy in America, 1860–1880* (New York: Atheneum, 1969; orig. pub., 1935).

6.   Ira Berlin, Barbara J. Fields, Thavolia Glymph, Joseph P. Reidy, and Leslie S. Rowland, eds., *Freedom: A Documentary History of Emancipation, 1861–1867*, ser. 1, vol. 1, *The Destruction of Slavery* (Cambridge: Cambridge Univ. Press, forthcoming).

7.   See Louis S. Gerteis, *From Contraband to Freedman: Federal Policy Towards Southern Blacks, 1861–1865* (Westport, Conn.: Greenwood Press, 1973); On the black military experience, see Du Bois, *Black Reconstruction*; Benjamin Quarles, *The Negro in the Civil War* (Boston: Little, Brown, 1953); James M. McPherson, *The Negro's Civil War: How American Negroes Felt and Acted during the War for Union* (New York: Pantheon, 1965); Dudley Taylor Cornish, *The Sable Arm: Negro Troops in the Union Army, 1861–1865* (New York: Norton, 1966; orig. pub., 1956); and Ira Berlin, Joseph P. Reidy, and Leslie Rowland, eds., *Freedom: A Documentary History of Emancipation, 1861–1867*, ser. 2, *The Black Military Experience* (Cambridge: Cambridge Univ. Press, 1982).

8.   Thomas C. Holt, "'An Empire over the Mind': Emancipation, Race, and Ideology in the British West Indies and the American South," in *Region, Race, and Reconstruction*, ed. Kousser and McPherson, 286.

9.   The issue here, of course, is not that the question of land is or was unimportant, only that focusing upon it has tended to obscure the struggle of the former slaves where land was not available. In the American context, that was almost everywhere.

10.   Holt, "'An Empire over the Mind'," in *Region, Race, and Reconstruction*, ed. Kousser and McPherson, 285. See also E. P. Thompson, *The Making of the English Working Class* (New York: Pantheon, 1963), and Herbert G. Gutman, *Work, Culture, and Society in Industrializing America* (New York: Knopf, 1976).

11.   See also Woodman, "Sequel to Slavery," 549–54; "Post–Civil War Southern Agriculture and the Law," *Agricultural History* 53 (Jan., 1979): 317–37; and *King Cotton and His Retainers: Financing & Marketing the Cotton Crop of the South, 1800–1925* (Lexington: Univ. of Kentucky Press, 1968): 319–33.

12.   Hobsbawm, *Age of Revolution*.

13.   The term "unfreedom" comes from Thompson, *Making of the English Working Class*, 199.

ARMSTEAD L. ROBINSON

"Worser dan Jeff Davis": The Coming of Free Labor during the Civil War, 1861–1865

DURING the 1960s, a burst of new interest in studying the South's "peculiar institution" sparked a revival of concern about the configuration of society and economy in the postbellum South.[1] Since much of the scholarship in southern studies continues to draw its inspiration from C. Vann Woodward and Eugene Genovese, neo-consensus historians took a not altogether unexpected interest in the field, contesting the dominant role that Woodward and Genovese accord to social class as the primary factor shaping secular changes in nineteenth-century southern society. Out of this neo-consensus counterattack came the so-called "continuity" school, an approach best exemplified by Carl Degler's insistence that the fundamentals of southern society changed comparatively little throughout the nineteenth century.[2] Given the intensity of the debate over social class versus continuity as organizing principles, it seems clear that intensified research and writing in southern studies will continue for many years to come.

Advocates of southern "continuity" face the unenviable task of deemphasizing the impact upon the former Confederate States of their failed struggle for southern national independence. For despite neo-consensus assertions about the high degree of similarity in structure and functioning between antebellum and postbellum southern society, it does seem clear that the post–Civil War South differed in several critical ways from its prewar predecessor. In the first place, accepting southern "continuity" requires a willing suspension of disbelief on the question of whether defeat at the hands of the Yankees and the imposition of uncompensated emancipation produced fundamental alterations in the culture, ideology, and structure of the haughtily militant

This essay results from a research project generously funded by the University of California at Los Angeles Center for Afro-American Studies.

slaveholding society. Furthermore, it remains indisputable that post-war southern economic growth lagged far behind that of the rest of the United States, a performance that stands in stark contrast to the South's leading role throughout the antebellum period.[3] Unless we accept the dubious proposition that defeat, emancipation, and stunted economic growth exerted only insignificant influences on southern life and culture, it would appear that the outcome of the Civil War could not help but prepare the way for an era of revolutionary transformation within the South.

The search for insights into the character and direction of social change in the nineteenth-century South cannot avoid paying attention to the events of the Civil War era, particularly since those events set in motion social transformations that rendered the "New South" of Watterson and Grady virtually incomprehensible to the scions of the early national period's Virginia dynasty.[4] Defeat and emancipation mattered, since both resulted in significant diminution of southern sovereignty. Not only did the vanquished former Confederate States find themselves compelled to do the political bidding of their conquerors as the price for readmission into national politics, but emancipation also forced the South as a whole to accommodate itself to the disciplines of free labor. The simultaneous attempts to regain political comity and to resurrect the southern labor system would appear to constitute a discontinuity of sufficient magnitude to warrant describing the Civil War era as a period of revolutionary transformation for southern society.

This transformation involved nothing less than a sweeping redefinition of the structural relationships among and between the South's constituent social classes and racial groups. Harold Woodman focuses upon the essential point when he identifies emancipation as the most critical element calling forth this revolutionary process of social and economic change. Emancipation, Woodman argues, "required that former slaves learn to be free workers and that former masters learn to be employers." Because this process ensnared non-slaveholders from the southern backcountry as well as persons from the lowcountry, who were more directly attached to the orbit of the slaveholding economy, Woodman concludes that "we might profitably look at the period 1870 to 1900 as a time marked by the making of a working class from former slaves (and formerly self-sufficient whites) and the making of a bour-

geois employer class from former slaveowners."[5] Determining how
these processes of class formation realized themselves in the varied
milieus of the South's regional economies is the major challenge con-
fronting scholars concerned with explaining the character and direction of social change in the post–Civil War South.

Our comprehension of these postbellum developments might profit
from a focus on the Civil War itself, since revolutionary changes in the
southern labor system occurred simultaneously with the epic military
conflict between North and South. Benjamin Quarles offers a profound
insight when he insists that "by the time Lee's men had stacked their
muskets at Appomattox, Negroes everywhere had become free *de
facto.*"[6] If slaves throughout the Confederacy had won de facto freedom prior to the actual surrender, then it seems safe to suggest that
the revolutionary remaking of southern class structure found its origins
during, not *after*, the Civil War. While the origins of postbellum class
struggles could not determine the final outcome, these early experiences nonetheless do afford invaluable insights into the world views
and the expectations that former slaves, former masters, and northerners brought to the development of the postwar South.

I propose to examine certain aspects of the wartime experience
with the coming of free labor insofar as this wartime experience sheds
light on major trends in the development of postbellum society and
economy. The Mississippi Valley is my primary focus, with only limited
attention to the Atlantic coastal states. The Civil War wrought significant transformations within the labor systems of the Mississippi Valley's
many subregions. By looking at how slaves, masters, and northern invaders responded to these transformations, we can gain insight into
the factors that shaped regional variations in the transition from slavery to free labor. For example, although many Civil War blacks pressed
demands for wages, most of the freedpeople concentrated on the
struggle to gain economic independence through land ownership. In
short, freedom came to mean sharply different things to different
groups of freedpeople—depending on their personal situations, their
location, and the timing of formal emancipation—and this spectrum of
black perspectives on the meaning of freedom suggests that none of the
groups involved in the southern transition to free labor held a unitary
view. If neither the former slaves, the former masters, the yeomanry,
nor the Yankees brought a monolithic ideology to the task of reconsti-

tuting southern labor systems, then the half-century of experimentation and conflict that followed the Civil War takes on suggestive new meanings.

I

No discussion of black labor during the Civil War could begin without acknowledging our debt to the pioneers in this field. Two books published amid the agonies of the Great Depression set standards for scholarship and charted paths for analysis to which contemporary scholars can return with great benefit. Bell Irvin Wiley's *Southern Negroes: 1861–1865* and W. E. B. Du Bois's *Black Reconstruction in America, 1860–1880* remain the indispensable starting points for a study of the wartime transformation of the southern labor system.[7] Du Bois led the way by insisting upon the need to conceptualize the coming of free labor as a struggle arising out of conflicts between the interests of the landed versus those of the landless classes, and Wiley followed up by patiently mining widely scattered manuscript repositories. Taken together, these contributions continue to inform contemporary scholarship, since they lay out the groundwork for both the description and the analysis of the wartime origins of a southern free labor economy.

Both Du Bois and Wiley emphasized the importance of timing and location. Wiley made an important point when he insisted on the distinctive wartime experiences within "interior" versus "exterior" slaveholding areas. According to Wiley, the disruptive effects that the Civil War produced within southern labor systems reached their peak in those areas closest to the invading northern army.[8] While this perspective understates the significant inroads that occurred behind Confederate lines, the fact remains that whenever northern soldiers appeared, their presence struck the "peculiar institution" a death blow. Similarly, Du Bois argued that black laborers undertook what amounted to a "general strike" in response to Lincoln's Emancipation Proclamation.[9] Even if the concept of a general strike exaggerates the degree of wartime communication between widely scattered groups of slaves, the activities of these groups often reflected an unexpectedly sophisticated comprehension of the value of collective action as a tool in obtaining control over their labor and over its fruits. By sensitizing scholars to the significance of time and place in the coming of free labor, Du Bois and Wiley made a critical contribution to any analysis of the wartime antecedents of postbellum social change.

Emphasizing the impact of time and place requires fairly careful specification of when, where, and how freedom came to slaves in the Mississippi Valley. The region first occupied by the northern army included the areas where antebellum modifications of slave management practices had laid the broadest foundations for slaves' rudimentary contact with the disciplines of free labor. The border states of Kentucky, Missouri, and western Virginia comprised the first portions of slave-holding territory permanently resecured for the Union. In these regions, antebellum slaveholders had tended to employ their slaves in the production of hemp and tobacco, and on farms that engaged in mixed cultivation of grain and livestock. Since these were the systems of production in which non-gang labor and individualized hiring out were most common,[10] the northern invaders encountered there a number of single black males who seemed quite comfortable exchanging their labor power for wages, particularly if such an exchange helped secure their claim to freedom prior to the effective implementation of emancipation.

In southern Louisiana, the invaders encountered a superficially similar situation: slaves there, too, offered their services for hire; however, not only did the sheer numbers of escapees make a drastic difference, but these numbers also included women, children, and the elderly—groups that did not mesh smoothly with the single-sex organizational assumptions of the Union Army.

The full implications of this confrontation with the extended slave family did not become obvious until the spring of 1863, when the invaders attempted to implement emancipation during the Vicksburg campaign in the heart of the Cotton Kingdom. So rapidly did the numbers of slave escapees swell the noncombatant population dependent upon the Yankee invaders that the northern army found itself compelled to transfer control of custodial arrangements for the freedpeople first to civilian volunteers, then to the Treasury Department. Ultimately, this transfer produced the abandoned-plantation leasing scheme, a plan that introduced the concept of free labor to hundreds of thousands of Mississippi Valley blacks.[11]

As enormous as were the numbers of black refugees, an even larger number of Mississippi Valley slaves obtained their initial contact with freedom while remaining on or near their prewar residences. Louis Gerteis estimates that during the entire Civil War, up to one million blacks lived within the areas controlled by the northern army.[12] Since this is only one-quarter of the roughly four million slaves counted by the 1860 United States census, the majority of blacks who gained de facto freedom by war's end must have done so in small and painfully won increments, as their freedom of action expanded to fill the vacuum left by the contraction of their masters' dominance.[13] Because the Cotton Kingdom encompassed the vast majority of antebellum slaves, the "interior" regions least affected by the wartime presence of northern soldiers may well have provided the most important arena for initial exposure to the coming of free labor. The evidence suggests that even in these more isolated areas, the complex processes whereby free labor came to life as slavery died produced far-reaching changes in the labor regime, changes that foreshadowed significant trends in the postbellum economy.

By focusing first on the border states, then on southern Louisiana, and finally on the Cotton Kingdom, it will be possible to sketch out the broad parameters of the wartime advent of free labor in the Mississippi Valley, and the significant social conflict that arose out of the often incompatible class interests of the landed and the landless throughout the valley's slaveholding regions. On one side stood the slaves, who by and large expected their northern liberators to take their part in confrontations over the meaning of freedom. On the other side stood the masters, who quite properly saw emancipation as a fundamental challenge to their control over the slaves' labor power. Caught in the middle was the invading army. Since the Yankees had not anticipated that their arrival would precipitate such a massive defection of blacks, they were not prepared to resolve the resulting struggles between masters and slaves. Predictably, the invaders found it easier to come to terms with the interests of landowning former slaveholders seeking to obtain faithful labor than with the interests of landless freedpeople determined to assert their right to control their own labor power. Thus many aspects of the Civil War experience with the coming of free labor foreshadowed the rapprochement ultimately achieved between northern and southern commercial interests—an accord rooted in the commonality of concerns between upper-class groups both North and South.[14]

II

When President Lincoln dispatched northern units into the border states during the spring and summer of 1861, few within the War Department had considered how attractive an invading army might appear to the slaves there. Apparently, the northern high command expected the blacks to remain passive while white men fought over the question of southern independence. These expectations would prove erroneous in several ways: not only did tens of thousands of slaves rush toward the northern army, but many members of the Union detachments refused to comply with orders to return fugitive slaves to their owners. As a result, the question of how to deal with runaway slaves continued to plague Lincoln and his commanders throughout the war.[15]

Attempting to retain the loyalty of the upper South's slaveholding states, Lincoln and his generals believed it critically important to reassure slaveowners in border states remaining within the Union that the northern army intended no interference with the "peculiar institution." Senior officers accepted the President's contention that the army would do well to separate itself from the troublesome questions posed by the presence of runaway slaves. Accordingly, they issued orders directing subordinates to prevent runaways from using northern camps as places of refuge.

Typical of the effort to accomplish the dual task of discouraging runaways and reassuring slaveholders was a circular issued on July 4, 1861, by the commander of an Ohio regiment serving in western Virginia under General George B. McClellan: "As our enemies have belied our mission and reported us a band of abolitionists, I desire to assure you that the relation of master and servant as recognized in your State will be respected. . . . I assure you that those under my command have preemptory orders to take up and hold any negroes found running about camp without passes from their masters."[16] And in November, 1861, General Henry Halleck, overall commander of northern forces in the border states, went so far as to issue a General Order directing that fugitive slaves not be "permitted to enter the lines of any camp . . . and that any now within the lines be immediately excluded therefrom."[17]

Problems surfaced quickly, however, because a number of volunteer officers expressed ethical reservations about returning fugitive slaves to their owners. Unlike some members of the regular army's officer corps, many civilian volunteers found it strangely contradictory that the North would use free labor ideology as a justification for making war against a slaveholding power and at the same time institute policies that had the practical effect of undercutting that ideology by sending fugitives back to involuntary labor. So abhorrent did Colonel John Beatty find this practice that he confided to his diary in July 1861: "I believe the war will run into a war of emancipation, and when it ends, African slavery will have ended also. It would not perhaps be politic to say so, but if I had the army in my own hands, I would take a short cut to what I am sure will be the end—commence the work of emancipation at once, and leave every foot of soil free behind us."[18]

In August, 1861, one senior officer did precisely what Beatty suggested: General John C. Frémont issued an emancipation proclamation affecting both Kentucky and Missouri. Unfortunately for General Frémont, Lincoln took keen exception to the decree; he not only revoked the proclamation but removed Frémont from command.[19]

Still, nothing stemmed the flow of runaway slaves toward northern lines or reduced blacks' enthusiasm for freedom and their readiness to offer whatever assistance they could to the northern invaders. A Union officer reported from Kentucky in October, 1861: "Boys growling about their supper tonight. . . . Some darkies bring us buttermilk."[20] As his regiment moved with Grant's invading army, General Lew Wallace reported on almost a full year's experience with similar receptions throughout the border states. "There is no denying the fact that the negroes believe we came as their deliverers," said Wallace in a letter to his wife. "Sight of us affords them absolute joy. . . . In vain their mistresses tell them of our barbarities. The blacks persist in being glad and in betraying them."[21]

Complementing the slaves' persistent pursuit of freedom was the growing reliance among northern soldiers upon the service that blacks could render. Alan Pinkerton, during his travels as a Yankee spy in the summer of 1861, reported, "I found that my best source of information was the colored men, who were employed in various capacities of a military nature."[22] Although comparatively few slaves participated in the high adventure of spying, significant numbers of runaways did per-

form camp chores, thereby relieving many northern soldiers of drudgery. As one private saw it, "One of the most important things is that we
have a negro servant and I tell you that *it makes a considerable difference in the domestic part of camp life.*"[23]

Union officers and soldiers stationed at duty posts across the upper
South were startled to discover that many of these blacks demanded
payment in cash for their services. In August, 1861, Colonel Beatty's
regiment encountered black male fugitives in the western Virginia
mountains who demanded compensation for camp labor.[24] And from
Middle Tennessee, Private Cyrus Boyd reported, "This morning the
camp was alive with colored men, women and children, hunting situations in the Brigade as cooks or any kind of servants for 'de Union
Boys'."[25] Almost any northern unit entering the upper South's slaveholding regions could expect to be approached by blacks, usually young
and male, who anxiously sought employment. So common did the
practice of hiring them become that town leaders along Kentucky's
Ohio River border with the "free" states of Indiana and Ohio complained bitterly about the highly visible numbers of blacks passing
through their towns in the company of northern units being rotated
out of the war zone.[26]

Indeed, so long as most northern generals continued to comply
with Lincoln's hands-off policy vis-à-vis runaway slaves, it made good
sense for black escapees to secure their safety by cementing a relationship with a northern soldier, particularly a commissioned officer. Perceptive officers recognized the craftiness displayed by many runaways.
As Major William Thompson, serving in western Missouri in the fall of
1861, commented in response to a friend's query about blacks' capabili-
ties for adjustment to a life in freedom, "They are just as sharp as their
masters and much more cunning. It would surprise you to see the
numbers that are here now, all wanting a place, where he [*sic*] may
earn something and be with the army. Many of the females . . . are
importuning us everyday to go as washerwomen or any kind of work to
be done."[27] Although such unequal power relationships imposed a predictable if unfortunate burden of fraud and abuse upon the freedpeople, thousands of *unattached* young slaves nonetheless took advantage of the northern presence in the upper South to seek freedom and
employment. The apparent facility with which they translated freedom

from slavery into freedom to demand wages probably reflected the impact of extensive self-hiring as well as the practice of incentive payments to encourage more purposeful labor from the slaves.

On the other hand, few indeed were the heads of slave families who seemed willing to risk the safety of their relatives by running away and leaving them to the tender mercies of vengeful masters. It was not until mid-1864, when the North promised freedom to families of black enlistees, that Kentucky and Missouri experienced really massive freedom escapes. Until then, the erosion of border state slavery occurred within the context of small, widely scattered slaveholding units where the authority of the master rested on his ability to evoke individual submission from each of the slaves. The result was a much more individualistic assertion of free labor rights than occurred in either southern Louisiana or in the Cotton Kingdom. Because the border states' postbellum economy moved so rapidly toward a deemphasis upon the role of black labor in tobacco and hemp production, it would prove considerably easier for border state blacks to filter north across the Ohio and west toward Kansas and the Great Plains.[28]

III

Almost a full year after northern armies entered the border states, an invasion force under the command of General Benjamin Butler captured the city of New Orleans. The fall of New Orleans brought the Union cause face to face with a quantitatively and qualitatively different situation from that presented by action in the upper South. Not only were there far greater numbers of blacks in the immediate vicinity of the Crescent City than anywhere in Kentucky, but the organization of the sugar plantations that dominated the regional economy was radically different from that of the smaller holdings of the border states.. With slaveholdings of over a hundred blacks quite common throughout the region south of Baton Rouge, the invading army faced pressures unheard of during the Kentucky and Missouri campaigns.

Two additional factors made the situation in southern Louisiana significantly different: in August, 1861, the northern Congress had passed the First Confiscation Act; in March 1862, the Congress enacted a new article of war, specifically prohibiting northern troops from using armed force to return fugitive slaves to their masters.[29] Equally important were the heightened political activities of northern abolitionists who advocated converting the war to save the Union into a war to destroy slavery.[30] These developments apparently encouraged volunteer officers and soldiers to resist Lincoln's fugitive slave policy even more openly than had been the case in the border states; thus, blacks attracted by the presence of Butler's army found it easier than might otherwise have been expected to arrange "situations" within northern camps.

No one seemed fully prepared for the crush of fugitives who would attempt to gain freedom by escaping to areas controlled by Butler's troops. To his credit, Butler had an inkling of the problems that might arise, since it was he who had commanded at Fortress Monroe, Virginia, when the first "contrabands of war" sought both protection and freedom beneath the cover of northern guns.[31] Perhaps because Lincoln knew of Butler's earlier role in allowing runaway slaves into the lines, the President called the general aside after their last strategy session prior to Butler's embarkation for Louisiana. Lincoln told him, Butler recalled, that "the government was not yet prepared to announce a negro policy. . . . He must 'get along' with the negro question as best he could, endeavor to avoid raising insoluble problems and sharply defining issues; and try to manage so that neither abolitionist nor conservatives would find in his acts occasion for clamor."[32] In short, Lincoln left Butler on his own, after ordering him to handle the fugitive slave question as best he could so long as his policies did not spark partisan debate.

Blacks in southern Louisiana responded to the presence of northern soldiers with enthusiasm similar to that expressed by slaves in the border states. Even the most casual observation of the reception given the northern fleet, as it steamed toward New Orleans after the victories at Fort St. Phillip and Fort Jackson, indicated the scope of the refugee problem soon to confront General Butler. Captain John DeForrest saw an elderly black woman who shouted loudly at the passing flotilla, "Bless de Lawd! I knows dat ar flag. I knew it would come. Praise de Lawd!"[33] A Wisconsin-born private who rode with DeForrest described this reception in even more suggestive terms:

> For the first time in my life I saw a gang of field hands at work. They were hoeing sugar cane and had an overseer with them with his long whip (a negro by the way). As we passed they looked up very whistful [sic] but did

not dare to say anything. I noticed this one little negro, however, get behind a large bush and there wave his hat like fury. As we passed different
gangs where the overseer was away, the negroes would point to the Stars
and Stripes and wave their hats. All too often some old fellow would throw
his hat on the ground and put his foot on it while pointing at our flag. For a
long while we couldn't make out what it meant, but finally a negro on board
said they meant to tell us they were glad the old flag had come back and
that their masters wouldn't *dare* to use them so bad.[34]

Apparently, these blacks believed that the arrival of the northern fleet
meant the end of involuntary servitude and the beginning of free labor.

In the aftermath of the fall of New Orleans, the federal government
experienced an unwelcome foretaste of the difficult situation that would
ensue once Lincoln made emancipation a formal war aim. It did not
take very long for an enormous crush of fugitive slaves to descend on
Butler's camp outside of New Orleans; within six weeks of his arrival,
Butler found that more than ten thousand blacks had made their way
through the northern lines. The general blanched at the thought of
caring for such a crush of humanity. In response to a query from Secretary of War Edwin Stanton about whether his army could provide food
and shelter for all the slaves able to evade the Confederate cavalry pa-
trols, Butler insisted, "*It is a physical impossibility to take all.* I cannot
feed the white men within my lines." Warming to the task, the general
asserted melodramatically, "Women and children are actually starving
despite all I can do. Aye, and they too without fault on their part. What
would be the state of things if I allowed all the slaves from the plantations to quit their employment and come within our lines is not to be
conceived of by the imagination."[35]

The general, concluding that his only hope lay in dissuading additional fugitives from fleeing to his lines, ordered his soldiers to refuse
shelter to any more slave runaways, apparently believing that such a
move would compel the blacks to remain on their plantations. However, the Massachusetts-born Democrat failed to make adequate allowance for two critical factors: the blacks' determination to gain freedom,
and his own soldiers' sympathetic response to slave escapees.

Captain DeForrest's account illustrates how difficult a task General
Butler was undertaking. Within days of his arrival at New Orleans,
DeForrest entered into negotiations that transformed a fugitive slave
into a hired camp servant. After less than three weeks, DeForrest con-

sidered his new employee safe from repatriation: "His master would have a deuce of a time reclaiming him from the Brigade Commander who clutches at every opportunity of humiliating slave owners and rebels." Matters reached such a state that the entire membership of the 13th Connecticut Infantry Volunteers resolved in a meeting never to remand a fugitive to his owner, no matter what General Butler said. "The owners go to the General and beg for their ebony chattels. The General sends for the captains of the 13th and requests them to let the people go. The captains argue that the girls want to wash and get paid for it, and that the regulations allow 40 washerwomen to a battalion of ten companies. There the matter invariably ends."[36]

This situation quickly escalated into an open confrontation. General John Wolcott Phelps, commanding northern forces at Fort Parapet where DeForrest was stationed, refused to obey a special order from General Butler allowing "loyal" slave masters to reclaim runaways from Union camps. In fact, Phelps's men went so far as to liberate a slave fugitive from the custody of a New Orleans police detachment, thereby making a free man out of a slave accused of the capital offense of arson.[37] General Butler exploded with rage, both at this particular incident and at the blatant contempt Phelps's men generally displayed towards his orders. Butler took his complaints directly to Secretary of War Stanton, only to discover that Lincoln meant what he said when he asked Butler not to allow his fugitive slave policy to become a subject of partisan controversy. Rather than confront the issue directly, Stanton counseled Butler to allow it to pass.[38] Apparently, this advice extended as well to Phelps's refusal to expel "unemployed" runaway slaves from his camp.[39] As a result, ever larger numbers of fugitives came to the lines near New Orleans, creating an even more desperate crisis among the thousands of black refugees.

General Butler took advantage of this crisis to propose a "temporary" solution that carried the complementary consequence of providing many Louisiana blacks with their first sustained exposure to free labor. After claiming that "the blacks . . . are coming by hundreds, nay thousands, daily," Butler suggested that "unemployed" fugitives be hired out as contract laborers on plantations operated either by local slaveholders or by northern lessees.[40] Expediency found a rival in profit as a motive for this action. In addition to alleviating the refugee problem, the contract labor scheme also promised to provide much of the labor to produce the cotton and sugar so desperately needed by New England industry. Caught up, perhaps, by the spirit of capitalist benevolence in which he presented this program of refugee relief, General Butler professed to see nothing improper about leasing a plantation to his brother, Andrew Jackson Butler, even though Andrew Butler managed, with the assistance of northern troops, to make a small fortune in only four months.[41] Not only did General Butler find the plantation leasing scheme effective and profitable, but his successor, General Nathaniel Banks, also discovered that this "temporary" solution worked well enough to serve as the principal mechanism for coping with black refugees for the balance of the war.[42]

Unfortunately, the system involved considerable coercion, even though the formal rules drafted by Butler prohibited the use of physical force to elicit labor. The runaways cared but little for a return to life on the plantations, and loyal slaveholders and northern lessees soon discovered that Louisiana blacks expected freedom from slavery to mean the birth of a regime in which the laborers possessed a significant degree of independent control over the terms and conditions under which they would work. In the conflict that emerged between the landowners' interest in profit maximization and the laborers' interest in reasonable work conditions and fair compensation, wartime plantation managers found it necessary to employ harsher and harsher measures in order to suppress demands for better working conditions and higher wages. In fact, so widespread did resistance to contract labor become that many plantations received semipermanent detachments of Union soldiers to assist in controlling the black work force.[43]

This development precipitated a new confrontation between Butler and Phelps. Phelps objected strenuously to orders directing him to use soldiers from the free states to compel blacks to accept conditions that he viewed as synonymous with slavery. Such duty seemed particularly onerous because many of those calling for assistance were slaveholders enmeshed in labor struggles with their former slaves. "The question now," Phelps argued, "is whether the particular interests of the government are to be brought into accord with the particular interests of the slaveholders or whether the particular interests of the slaveholders are to be made subordinate to the government."[44] Unfortunately for the interests of the former slaves, the northern War Department refused to sustain Phelps's position in his dispute over the use of federal troops as bullyboys for the contract labor system.

When Phelps realized that he could do nothing to prevent the exploitation of black laborers, he resigned. "Tendered my resignation yesterday," he noted in his diary, "unconditional and immediate— rather than become a slave driver. Party is made for man and not man for party. The Union as it was and the Constitution as it is with liberty as the intention of the instrument and not slavery."[45]

These eloquent sentiments stand in sharp contrast to the actions of another northern army officer who intervened in a labor dispute in July, 1862. Although General Butler's contract labor system promised "generous" compensation and fair treatment for the blacks, conditions grew so poor on a plantation near Donaldsonville, Louisiana, that the blacks went on strike to protest mistreatment, inadequate provisions, and nonpayment of wages. Their prewar owner responded to this brand of free labor activism by appealing for assistance to the northern provost marshall. When the blacks involved in the work stoppage saw a gunboat bearing the Stars and Stripes, they rushed to welcome their liberators. However, instead of seeking to determine the legitimacy of the freedpeople's grievances, the officer in charge demanded to know the identity of the strike leaders. When several black men stepped forward, the northern officer had them bound, arrested, and placed in the plantation stocks. Afterward, the officer proceeded to lecture the assembled slaves about the meaning of "free labor": that is, their obligation to honor contracts. An elderly black man who witnessed the entire scene watched in utter confusion and amazement at the direction in which northern preferences for planters' class interests could take the wartime experiment with free labor. Sick at heart, this former slave turned away, muttering under his breath, "Dis here is more worser dan Jeff Davis."[46]

Not all of the confrontations between laborers and landowners ended quite so sadly. In late September, the blacks on Magnolia Plantation in Placquemines Parish, Louisiana, asked their former owner to pay them ten dollars a month per hand, in addition to providing food, clothing, and shelter. The owner, Effingham Lawrence, found these terms preposterous. When he declined to accede to their requests, his steward reported that a "woman strike" began the next day: female field hands returned to their cabins after the noon meal, declining to return to work until Lawrence agreed to their wage demands. The work stoppage spread quickly as the male field hands followed the women's lead. When Lawrence still refused to reach an agreement, a group of the freedpeople, under cover of darkness, constructed a gallows outside the steward's cabin. When asked why they had undertaken so drastic an action, the freedpeople told their astonished questioner that the "Yankees" had ordered them to do it. Apparently, the specter of this hastily constructed but quite functional gallows softened Lawrence's resolve; although he still refused to pay "wages" to his blacks, he did promise a "handsome present" if they worked faithfully through the fall grinding season. Sure enough, at the end of three months, Lawrence gave his eighty former slaves a quite handsome present of $2,400[47]—thus saving face by describing as a "handsome present" what was in fact the requested wage settlement.

A number of factors generally not present in the Cotton Kingdom enabled groups of Louisiana blacks to employ collective action. In the first place, the very nature of the preindustrial sugar industry, with its land-extensive and labor-intensive cultivation and processing regimens, had virtually ensured that slaveholders would organize estates with very large work forces.[48] And because the swampy areas in which cane grows best posed a major health hazard for whites, sugar planters had felt themselves compelled to use blacks as drivers and even overseers much more often than was the norm for the South as a whole. During the war, black drivers often turned against their former masters; Governor Thomas Moore reacted with shock and horror to a report that during an invasion of Alexandria, Louisiana, "the drivers *everywhere* have proved the worst negroes."[49] Thus, it should not be altogether surprising that slaves quartered in large numbers on plantations organized with blacks in supervisory positions might achieve a higher level of disciplined labor action than those working in other types of labor systems. In a different sort of collective action, a significant number of multigenerational extended kin groups simply squatted on abandoned land during the war, thereby experiencing freer labor than many of them were ever likely to find again.[50]

For the balance of the war, tens of thousands of Louisiana blacks lived and worked as contract laborers on leased plantations. In most instances, they found themselves victimized by vandal capitalists like

Andrew Butler, who sought to exploit the short-term artificial situation created by the war. With sugar in short supply and with labor overly abundant near northern posts, wartime lessees could extract maximum profits with little regard for the long-run health of the estates they leased. And while sugar plantations seemed ideally suited for gang labor with an agrarian proletariat, these plantations remained quite vulnerable to collective action of the kind practiced successfully at Magnolia Plantation. So long as a strike during grinding season could wipe out an entire year's production, the risks of operating a commercial sugar plantation remained quite high. This vulnerability and the reluctance of freedpeople to return to antebellum levels of labor intensity may help to explain why the postbellum Louisiana sugar industry never recovered from the shock administered by defeat and emancipation.[51] In any case, the wartime experiment with free labor in Louisiana did foreshadow the conflicts between landless laborers and landed plantation owners that would continue to bedevil the postbellum southern economy until well into the twentieth century.

IV

The Vicksburg campaign gave Grant's army an opportunity to implement the Emancipation Proclamation in the heart of the Mississippi Valley's Cotton Kingdom. Quite predictably, this effort precipitated a rapid erosion of antebellum labor relations, but its pace stunned the invaders as well as the resident slaveowners. Not only did the northern army find itself overwhelmed by the sheer numbers of freedom-seeking blacks, but the masters discovered that they could not regain control over their slaves unless they abandoned their plantations and fled to the Confederate "interior." Their flight provided the Yankees with productive land upon which to create an effective mechanism for coping with the multifaceted dilemmas created by emancipation. Again, northern lessees took over many of these abandoned plantations, using black laborers supplied by the Union army. Conditions on these plantations remained far from ideal, since many lessees refused to honor their promises about working conditions and living arrangements. Because no group seemed either willing or able to assume the burden of caring for unemployed slave refugees, it fell to other blacks to pay for the meager care these fugitives received—through a tax levied by the Yankees against the employed blacks' wartime earnings from growing cotton. Out of this experience would come the painful discovery that free laborers stood little chance in competition against the combined interests of planters and northern industrialists.

The Vicksburg campaign occurred in three major phases. Initially, a combined land-sea force attempted to compel the city to surrender. However, unlike the people of New Orleans, Baton Rouge, and Natchez, who surrendered in preference to seeing their cities turned into battlefields, Vicksburg's residents refused to submit without a fight to the finish. Northern commanders attempted a number of expedients, including the construction of a canal to bypass the blufftop citadel. When none of these strategies worked, the expedition withdrew in July, 1862, after a two-month stay in the river opposite the city. Not until late November, 1862, did the Union mount another sustained assault. This time, Grant attempted a pincers movement, with one arm traveling overland from Memphis while the other moved by water. Unfortunately for Grant, his Confederate adversaries managed to sever the extended supply line linking the overland segment to its forward bases. Accordingly, Grant withdrew, leaving Sherman to fight an inconclusive engagement at Chickasaw Bluffs, north of Vicksburg. This second setback persuaded Grant that Vicksburg would fall to only one kind of strategy: a prolonged close-order investment. In January, 1863, therefore, he shifted his headquarters to the swampy Louisiana shore opposite Vicksburg and devoted the next six months to probing the city's defense. On May 17, Grant's army succeeded in laying siege to Vicksburg, the siege that eventually produced the July 4th surrender that opened the Mississippi River cotton belt to the full effects of the northern emancipation weapon.[52]

This third phase of the Vicksburg campaign occurred simultaneously with the initial portion of the northern attempt to implement the Emancipation Proclamation. However, even before reaching the cotton heartland, Grant had already discovered that far greater numbers of slaves wished to avail themselves of freedom than the northern army could possibly use effectively. Seeking to rid his camps of surplus blacks, Grant contracted with a northern labor recruiter to send refugee blacks to midwestern cities. This gambit evoked an immediate and heated rebuff from the Lincoln administration, which insisted that the specter of black refugees surging toward the North created a political blacklash that threatened to undermine support for the war effort. Grant learned what Butler had already discovered: that Lincoln meant to contain the dilemmas created by wartime runaways within the southern states.[53]

A policy issue of this magnitude called for high-level consultation. In January, 1863, Lincoln met with Stanton and Navy Secretary Gideon Welles to thrash out the complex set of political and social problems raised by the decision to implement emancipation. Subsequently, Stanton acted on Lincoln's orders and directed the Adjutant General of the Army, Lorenzo Thomas, to go to the Mississippi Valley and take charge of implementing emancipation. General Thomas undertook the lengthy journey to Grant's headquarters without a formal plan of action, armed only with Lincoln's instructions that whatever formula he devised should involve the least possible political repercussion in the free states. General Thomas understood the dual thrust of Lincoln's plan; the northern President saw emancipation as a double-edged weapon, one that would weaken the Confederacy by draining away valuable laborers and also strengthen the North by providing a hitherto untapped source of manpower for the Union army. Thomas knew of the experiences at Fortress Monroe, Virginia, in the South Carolina Sea Islands, and in southern Louisiana, which showed that the invading army could attract large numbers of black fugitives only at the cost of providing shelter for multigenerational extended families.

By the time he reached Cairo, Illinois, General Thomas had drafted a preliminary plan of action, which he sent to Washington for perusal by the Secretary of War and the President. Accepting the conventional political wisdom that moving freedmen north would be impolitic, Thomas couched his solution in free labor rhetoric. The blacks flocking to the northern lines, Thomas asserted, "should be put into a position to make their own living. The men should be employed as laborers and teamsters and those who could be induced to do so or conscripted if necessary, be mustered into the service as soldiers, and the others with the women and children placed on abandoned plantations to till the ground."[54]

This rudimentary plan of action provided the basic framework for free labor adjustments among black refugees for the balance of the Civil War. In practice, it resulted in dividing the black population into three discrete groups. The first group included the able-bodied men who found themselves either drafted into the federal army or working as military laborers. The second encompassed the families of men serving the northern government; this group tended to take up residence on abandoned plantations, working as contract laborers under wage guidelines established by General Thomas. The sick and elderly who constituted the third major group tended to end up on Freedmen's Home Farms, wretched disease-ridden contraband camps paid for by taxes levied on the wages of other freedpeople.

All of these arrangements required time to establish. During the interval between Thomas's presentation of his plan and its full-scale implementation, northern soldiers encountered a reception similar to those met in the border states and in southern Louisiana: enthusiastic blacks were anxious to avail themselves of freedom and the opportunity to earn money in the process. Near Grant's headquarters at Lake Providence, Louisiana, "at least forty niggers came to me," reported an Iowa doctor, Senneca Thrall, "hat off 'Massa don you wan a boy to take care of your hoss, black you boots, do anything you want, oh Massa, take me with you, do take me with you'." [55]

It did not take long for many fugitives to conclude that the freedom they experienced in disease-ridden shanties and ragged tents erected around the peripheries of northern army camps bore scant resemblance to the Day of Jubilo about which they had dreamed for so long. In addition to the physical rigors of life in the camps, the blacks also discovered that a number of their Yankee friends proved harsh taskmasters, demanding even more work than had the slaveowners.

So disillusioned were the freedpeople that quite significant numbers of them ran away from the Yankees, preferring life on the old home place or maroonage to overwork and abuse at the hands of their supposed liberators. An Iowa soldier charged with supervising one group expressed bitter resentment when confronted by this particular method of collective action: "About three days ago I had 21 turned over to me who were taken from plantations in Alabama, and today after working but three days, they have begged me half the day to give them passes to go home. . . . I told them if they went they better stay and never show me their faces again." [56]

Not surprisingly, freedmen viewed these situations in a sharply different light. Frank Smith cogently expressed the dissatisfaction that many blacks felt about working for the Union army; he disliked "Yankees" because "dey wanted you to wuk *all de time*."[57] Other freedpeople found cause for discontent in their failure to receive the wages promised by their northern friends. One freedman ran away from the Yankees back to his former master. When asked how much money he received in payment for his months of labor as a camp servant, the former fugitive expostulated bitterly, "Never a cent. Oh the mean rascal.—Just like a Yankee."[58] Running away from the Yankees provided one means of obtaining relief from military labor demands that conflicted with freedmen's sense of what "free labor" ought to entail.

Running away also provided a means of contesting strange Yankee notions that once a person agreed to work for wages, that person incurred an obligation to continue doing so, regardless of his or her other interests. A northern officer gave unwitting testimony to the divergent cultural assumptions that freedpeople often brought to their initial experiences with free labor: "Ball's servant . . . does the cooking passably well and robs us to feed his friends and wives. . . . Lt. Berry's man . . . ran away several days ago. . . . These fellows work well and are fairly faithful until they are paid, when they seem to be taken with an irresistible desire to see the world."[59] It would appear that these freedmen wished to go into the nexus of free labor only far enough to gain for themselves and their dependents things that they could not obtain otherwise. Then, after earning whatever amount of money seemed adequate for their needs, they apparently wanted to retreat into working on their own initiative until such time as necessity again required a temporary sally into the cash economy.

The centrality of the ex-slaves' concern for the welfare of their dependents made a deep impression on General William Sherman. When officials at St. Louis requested the assignment of a number of blacks to work on the river, Sherman replied by insisting, "I appreciate the scarcity of labor . . . and doubt not that it could be remedied by employing negroes. . . . By opening the river to fugitive negroes, I believe we could send St. Louis any number by allowing them to take their families along."[60] Several months later a Sherman aide dispatched a similar reply to a request for black laborers for service on the Union river fleet. "General Sherman informs me that he can send you the 200 contrabands required, provided you are willing to receive their families with them. . . . The negroes are very averse to going further north. I have had the officers among them, endeavoring to recruit but with poor success."[61]

Concern for the security of their families prompted the heads of extended kin groups to exercise great caution about whether and when to make a break toward freedom with the Yankees. One of the women missionaries working with blacks from the Cotton Kingdom reported a striking example of the kind of reticence that was motivated by concern for the quality of life in the northern camps. When Laura Haviland asked the female leader of a recently arrived group of freedpeople whether she came in pursuit of freedom, the former slave replied:

> Freedom! . . . No, Missus, we never hear nothing like it. We's starvin' an' we come to get somfin' t'eat. Dat's what we come for. Our people home tell us Yankees want niggers to kill; an dey boils em up in great caldrons to eat, case dey's starvin'. But all de white men gone in de army, an' lef us wid missus, an dey locks de bacon up for de sojers, an' gib us little han'ful o' meal a day, a' we's got weak and trimbly. An' I tole my people we's gwine to die anyhow, an' we'd try de Yankees.[62]

Escapees fleeing the specter of starvation at home added considerably to the numbers of freedpeople with whom Grant's men found themselves compelled to contend. Since the northern government refused to appropriate any money for relief, the freedpeople themselves were forced to make involuntary contributions toward support of their indigent, elderly, and sick: a 10 percent tax was levied against the wages supposedly paid to black laborers and soldiers by the managers of leased plantations and also by the War Department. Reporting on his activities during 1864 as head of Mississippi Valley relief efforts for freedpeople, Chaplain John Eaton boasted about the success of this system of taxation: "Not a cent of money has ever been drawn from the Government, for the Freedmen on any account. A careful use of the tax required by Orders 63 and of funds accruing from the profits on labor in the departments, under the care of different superintendents, has met all the incidental expenses of these wide-spread operations."[63]

Chaplain Eaton also expressed pride in the performance of the small number of blacks to whom the northern government agreed to lease portions of abandoned plantations, particularly the settlement at Palmyra Bend, Mississippi, where Confederate President Jefferson

Davis owned one of the largest plantations. In both 1863 and 1864, the black drivers on the Davis plantations managed to earn large cash profits from the cultivation and sale of cotton.[64] Although Eaton recognized that the scale of wartime profitmaking at Palmyra Bend was exceptional, he believed that these activities merely hinted at the pool of entrepreneurial talent lurking among the freedpeople. His annual reports point to a number of examples,[65] and one of his assistants filed the following commentary on the success achieved by black lessees during the 1864 season:

> I cannot see that, in any particular, these colored men have been less successful than the white planters along side them. Where they employed hands, there is little if any complaint against them, either in the matter of rations or usage. Having undertaken small manageable tracts of lands, working them in good part themselves, and employing but a small number of hands, their crops have been more fully worked, so have produced more bountifully.[66]

It appears that the wartime experience with free labor revealed the beginnings of class differentiation *within* the community of freedpeople, a process that would exert significant impact upon postbellum southern political and social developments.

Perhaps nothing illustrated better the contrasting values and cultural assumptions held by the freedpeople and the Yankees than did the pride evident in Chaplain Eaton's dual boasts about black entrepreneurship on the one hand and black self-sufficiency on the other. Even though the makings of a black elite are clearly evident within the ranks of successful wartime entrepreneurs, it does seem obvious that the practical consequences of the system proposed by General Lorenzo Thomas and endorsed by Chaplain Eaton denied access to entrepreneurship for the vast majority of freedpeople. The abandoned-plantation scheme consigned wartime refugees to a life as tillers of soil owned by others. Put another way, that aspect of the coming of free labor that occurred beneath the aegis of the Yankees laid the basis for the creation of a postwar agrarian proletariat. Precisely because the victorious North could not bring itself to give former slaves anything more substantial than temporary use of land abandoned by Confederate supporters, postwar freedpeople would discover that they could not avoid compromising their deeply held desire for the economic autonomy of the extended family.

V

If the emancipation experience behind federal lines revealed the limitations of the northern commitment to free labor for southern blacks,
the analogous experience on the Confederate side exposed the inveter-
ate resistance to fully matured free labor relations that former slaveholders would express for many years after the Civil War. Members of
the master class seemed quite aware of the revolutionary alterations in
labor relations that followed in the wake of the war, and their reac-
tions belie claims for the "continuity" between ante- and postbellum
southern society. By examining how slaveholders responded to black
struggles for freedom during the war, we gain a perspective on the
problems that ensued once the military conflict came to an end. This
perspective suggests that the masters may have experienced greater
difficulty than the slaves in overcoming the psychological "heritage of
slavery."

In areas behind Confederate lines, the wartime demise of slave labor relations occurred in a number of different ways, with the precise
details of any scenario depending upon time and place and upon a particular slave's situation vis-à-vis the owner. One of the most surprising
venues for the birth of free labor appeared within Confederate army
camps. There, enterprising personal servants of affluent volunteers
discovered that they could take profitable advantage of their spare time
by selling or bartering their services to soldiers unable to afford a full-
time camp servant. The son of a Louisiana planter summed up the role
of Confederate body servants when he argued, "The negro was an im-
mense convenience to his master in that he did in general relieve the
latter of such domestic drudgery as cooking, washing, sewing, caring
for his horse, etc."[67] Another Louisiana plantation scion reported that
his servant Allen "has been and is getting on swimmingly." Allen did so
well that his master found out he was earning "a good deal of money for
his services" from poorer soldiers.[68] In fact, so proficient did Calib, the
body servant of Edward Burrus, become at making money in camp that
Burrus's father decided to stop sending Edward his allowance, urging
Edward to rely on Calib's earnings for pocket money.[69]

Less obvious but even more significant were the variety of ways
that slaves succeeded in playing their masters off against the southern
government. For example, the slaves of Nimrod Porter, a planter resid-

ing in Maury County, Tennessee, did Porter's bidding by evading a Confederate detachment seeking to impress blacks for labor in Confederate encampments. In return, Porter looked the other way while his "slaves" won significant concessions at home; as Porter put it, "Our negroes are getting along as usual only there is verry little in the way of working."[70] In another instance, a slave youth named Joe ran away from his west Tennessee owner during the spring of 1861. His master wrote the Confederate commander at Fort Randolph, Tennessee, requesting him to keep a sharp eye out for the runaway "negro boy," whom the owner suspected would seek work as a waiter in one of the Confederate camps.[71] By playing anxious masters off against desperate Confederate officers, blacks in Confederate-held areas could substantially enlarge their margin of autonomy, even to the extent of gaining quasi-freedom with the tacit consent of either their owners or the southern army. This helps explain the fierce resistance that masters mounted to attempts by the southern government to use slave labor for military purposes.[72]

As the war progressed, it became increasingly apparent that the longer the conflict lasted, the less control owners would exert over their human property. Within two weeks after Mary Fitzpatrick's husband left their Alabama plantation for his duty post with the southern army, Mrs. Fitzpatrick dispatched an urgent note, demanding that her spouse return home "right away" in order to curtail the truculence of their newly restive blacks.[73] Another slaveholder's wife wrote from central Texas in August, 1863, about an incident that symbolized the general decline in control over slaves, even among those residing deep in the "interior." When an elderly master attempted to whip a prime fieldhand, the burly slave first scoffed contemptuously at the old man's feeble efforts and then refused to accept any punishment whatsoever. Adding insult to injury, the slave "cursed the old man all to pieces" as he walked but did not run to the woods, sending back word that he would return only if the slaveholder refrained from further attempts at correction. When the master assented to this new arrangement, a liberated person walked back to the plantation—certainly no longer a slave, even if he could not yet claim the full benefits of freedom.[74]

Neither male nor female owners reacted gracefully to the sudden disappearance of control over their slave property. Whether it came about because of the presence of northern troops or because of elevated levels of black assertiveness, the confrontation with free labor left many southern whites boiling with anger and resentment. Many felt themselves badly betrayed, since so much of the antebellum pro-slavery ideology had rested on the southern whites' confidence in the loyalty of their slaves, particularly their trusted domestic servants. How slaveholders reacted to the unwelcome advent of black assertiveness during the war tells us a great deal about how such persons might react in the immediate postbellum period.

Southern women responded quite negatively to the sudden absence of trusted slaves. Mrs. Mary Eskeridge expressed a familiar wartime complaint upon learning that three of her most valuable and trusted male slaves had escaped. "I have tried to do my part to the negroes," lamented Mrs. Eskeridge, "it is truly a trial of uprightness to own them. . . . Those *I trusted most* have deceived me most and will yet give me more trouble on account of their families."[75] The daughter of a plantation mistress commiserated with her sister about the depressing fashion in which their mother had responded to the disappearance of a trusted long-time personal servant: "I do wish Mama would bear it better but it is very hard at her age to train others."[76] The chores that now fell to former mistresses often stimulated expressions of rage; as a plantation mistress from Natchez put it, "John, Sarah and Rose have left and I did the washing for six weeks, came near ruining myself for life as I was too delicately raised for such hard work."[77]

Male slaveholders behaved little better when confronted with the unexpected disappearance of a favored slave. Judge Robert S. Hudson informed a friend, "My sickness still continues and since I wrote you I have lost two valuable servants. One young man the favorite of all the negroes I ever owned—He was more like a good friend than a servant to me in my feelings."[78] The Reverend Samuel Andrew Agnew vented in his diary the rage he felt when Wash, the plantation's trusted lead driver, decamped two days after the burial of Agnew's brother Luther. Since Wash had assisted Luther in managing the family estate, his disappearance struck a particularly damaging blow. Agnew responded with emotions of hurt and betrayal: "Wash has gone to the enemy. He is a great rascal, acting in this manner under the circumstances with which he was surrounded. He is an ungrateful and hypocritical wretch."[79]

Even when masters attempted to conceal the depth of their pain, the anguish caused by the loss of a trusted and experienced slave revealed itself all too clearly. Take the correspondence of a Mississippi slaveholder, G. W. Humphreys: "The oldest negro man I had and [the] one that my wife had entrusted with hiding her Queens ware and best bed clothing after dark hitched the mules to the wagon, took all that had been entrusted with him and his family which consisted in about 9—over half I had, and drove off. The balance I suppose have gone before this. (But this is a small matter.)"[80]

Few indeed were the wartime owners who could find it in their hearts to applaud the assertiveness of their former chattels. Since Humphreys plainly felt disinclined to provide his former slaves with a stake for their lives in freedom, his blacks, like many other groups of Civil War fugitives, took what they needed, apparently feeling that years of uncompensated toil entitled them to a concrete share of the fruits of their labor. In one particularly poignant instance, a planter followed his former slaves into a northern army camp, with the intention of persuading them to return to their former position on his west Tennessee cotton plantation. A Yankee soldier recorded the fashion in which these freedpeople responded: "One man who lost 56 negroes came into camp last night. Has 250 acres of cotton—cried about the niggers but they laughed. Strong men among the number also women old—middle aged—and young women—Babies etc. Twas an affecting sight I assure you. They took an old buggy and mule to haul their goods in."[81]

The reconstitution of the southern labor system could not await the outcome of the war,[82] since the population, both black and white, had to eat. If slaves responded to the wartime situation by redirecting their energies away from the tasks formerly assigned to them, then whites residing behind southern lines had to respond in some way to this new black initiative. The evidence suggests that whites began to forge new accommodations with their blacks, accommodations that reflected the changed balance of local forces wrought by the war. Masters and mistresses who wished to get any effective labor out of their blacks found themselves compelled to submit to new levels of personal and economic assertiveness. Symbolic of the situation is the flippant comment uttered by a female domestic whose mistress heard the doorbell and called out for the youthful slave to go down and open the door; the young woman replied tartly, "Answering bells is played out."[83] The mother of Confederate Senator Clement Clay encountered similar expressions of truculence on the family plantation near Huntsville, Alabama. Even though there were no Yankees in the immediate vicinity, the blacks, after learning about Lincoln's emancipation decree during the spring of 1863, decided that they would no longer heed the commands of the overseer. Mrs. Clay aptly summarized the new state of labor relations that prevailed throughout the wartime South when she wrote with mounting frustration, "The negroes are worse than free. They say they are free. We cannot exert any authority. I beg ours to do what little is done."[84]

Only by finding some means of eliciting *voluntary* cooperation, perhaps by paying wages or entering into equitable partnerships with their blacks, could Confederates obtain the labor power needed to grow essential foodstuffs. Despite repeated warnings from officials about the dangers that could arise from free labor experiments within the Confederacy, these experiments took place, motivated in large part by the urgent necessity of providing food for the civilian population. In fact, the legislatures in Arkansas, Mississippi, and Texas found these problems so widespread that they felt themselves compelled either to mandate rigid enforcement of antebellum prohibitions against slaves hiring out their own time or to enact new laws aimed at suppressing these seditious practices.[85]

Although such legislation might appear to indicate a tightening up of the labor system, its passage in fact reflected broad recognition of the irreparable damage already inflicted on the antebellum regime. The case of Mrs. Sarah D. Garrett is illustrative. In September, 1864, the Quarterly Court in Madison County, Mississippi, convicted Mrs. Garrett of "permitting her three slaves to go at large and trade as freemen." On the basis of Mississippi's new law, she was fined $500 and sentenced to one year in prison. Mrs. Garrett's appeal to the Governor for clemency offers a glimpse into the alterations wrought by three years of warfare:

> Your petitioner is a widow lady with a helpless family. Her negroes are her only support. . . . Her sons, her only protection, are in the army. . . . She has no person to control them and being thus situated, she became entirely dependent on her slaves, and was of necessity, to make them at all profitable, compelled to permit them to hire themselves. . . . The slave population has become much demoralized and difficult of management, your petitioner because of her widowed and helpless state chose rather to hire said slaves to themselves than to permit them to go at large as they could and probably would have done without any restraint or control over them.[86]

The judge who heard the case pleaded with Governor Charles Clark to commute her sentence, insisting that "the name and *fact* of imprisonment, however *short*, would be most mortifying and degrading to her feelings, and I think wholly unnecessary to the *arrest* of the evil *designed* to be remedied, so far as her case is *concerned.*"[87]

The Garrett case revealed the broad outlines of the truly revolutionary transformation that had taken place in southern labor relations, virtually unnoticed amid the thunder of the military struggle. For example, Governor Clark's decision to grant clemency to Mrs. Garrett produced a similar request for mercy in the case of a Lauderdale County man convicted under the same law. The district attorney who prosecuted the case requested clemency for Elisha Radford, arguing, "I know Mr. Radford to be a good and patriotic citizen, as he was convicted under a law not generally enforced and indeed not generally known. . . . He is a poor man and has two soldiers' families to support."[88] A southern woman put forward similar justifications in April of 1864; however, her Tennessee county court convicted her of violating state law when she allowed her slaves "to act as free men" and to "hire their own time."[89]

Lest we imagine that these were isolated instances unrepresentative of the general trend of labor relations within the wartime South, it is instructive to look at a major Confederate newspaper's evaluation. In July, 1863, the *Arkansas True Democrat* described the steady erosion in slaveholders' control over slave labor and summarized the widespread effects of this apparently uncontrollable trend: "Not withstanding stringent laws and ordinances against negroes hiring their own time, slaves hire houses and have cook shops, beer holes and other pretended means of support. They are flush of money; buy pistols and horses and get white men to bid for them at auctions. On Markham street, for two or three squares, every third house is a negro brothel where it is said whiskey is sold."[90]

Even in the most isolated "interior" regions of the Mississippi Valley, slaveholders could not escape confrontations with the wartime advent of free labor. To one mistress in central Texas, the news of Lincoln's victory in the 1864 presidential election foreshadowed an indefinite prolongation of the struggle for southern independence—and the specter of untold years of additional strife with her slaves prompted a stunning admission of the erosion of slave labor relations. "With the prospect of another four years war you may give your negroes away . . . and I'll move into a white settlement and work with my hands. . . . The negroes care no more for me than if I was an old free darkey and I get so mad sometimes I think I don't care . . . if Myles beats the last one of them to death. I can't stay with them another year alone."[91] Mrs. Anna Affleck discovered that she could not manage her Washington County, Texas, plantation in the absence of her husband and two sons. Indeed, she complained after her husband's departure, "In his absence I had a good deal of trouble with some of the negroes. . . . I would rather they go than feed and clothe them in their idleness."[92]

Mrs. Affleck's prayer that her newly obstreperous blacks might simply leave her in peace articulated the fondest hope of many wartime slaveowners caught in the wrenching transformation to a free labor economy. Everything about the new regime carried fearsome hints of adjustments that most former slaveholders preferred to avoid. Finalizing a contract required some form of negotiation, a process that conferred a glimmer of racial equality that many affluent white southerners found extremely difficult to accept. Discussions between former owners resentful of emancipation and former slaves jealous of their new freedoms brought predictable results. An observer in Tippah County, Mississippi, described one such scene: "McDonald (Dobbin's place) called his negroes to hire them a few days ago. His negroes declined contracting with him. He then drove them off from the place and has not a negro now."[93] Although driving assertive freedmen from the land might satisfy certain psychological needs, this tactic's ability to assure adequate labor had obvious limitations. Thus, like it or not, the realities of the transformation of the southern labor system required masters to enter into negotiations with former slaves.

Moreover, once a bargain was struck, it still remained for these mutually suspicious parties to work through a crop season and to settle up their accounts. The greater the percentage of prewar slaves who remained on a farm, the more dramatic was the setting when the slaveowner found him- or herself compelled for the very first time to square accounts and to pay blacks for agricultural labor. Giving incentive payments to one's slaves was not the same thing as paying wages to free laborers, since in the former arrangement the decision about whether to recognize superior performance remained a prerogative of the master, whereas in the latter the payment of an earned wage was a matter of right. The owner of a sugar plantation located on Bayou Lafourche, Louisiana, found it hard to concentrate completely on reckoning his cash liability to his former slaves; he considered that task "a disagreeable business."[94] So long as former owners balked at either negotiating contracts with their former slaves or settling up accounts, conflict would remain an inescapable part of the process of reconstructing a southern labor system.

Blacks seemed keenly aware of the difficulties that lay ahead of them. Even those with little experience in the intricacies of free labor recognized that the immediate postwar period would pose major challenges for persons without a strong claim to land. As the war wound down and Confederate defeat became inevitable, former slaves grew increasingly impatient about the absence of any firm commitment from the liberators to provide them with the basic prerequisite for economic independence: land. When the northern general in charge of the post at Fort Smith, Arkansas, attempted to follow his orders to compel the freedpeople to enter binding wage contracts for the 1865 growing season, one freedman found the prospect of permanent subjugation to wage labor so intolerable that he confronted the general directly about being emancipated from slavery into landless dependency. "I want some land; I am helpless," asserted the freedman. "You do nothing for me but give me my freedom." The flustered general felt himself in a quandary, since it seemed to him that the freedom to seek a job was a sufficient gift. The freedman responded from the depths of his culture when he insisted that this version of "free labor" was not the kind of freedom he wanted: "It is enough for the present; but I cannot help myself unless I get some land; then I can take care of myself and my family; otherwise I cannot do it."[95]

This freedman understood that landlessness thrust him into a hopelessly subordinate economic position. In this recognition we find answers to the question of why conflict prevailed throughout the economic reorganization of the postbellum South. Former slaves clearly hoped that freedom from chattel slavery would convey more than merely the extinguishing of their former masters' claims to ownership of their persons. They wanted the freedom to exercise economic independence, lest freedom from slavery provide little more than another form of involuntary servitude. This goal placed them on a collision course with the interests of landowning former slaveholders; only if the northern government had sided firmly and consistently with the freed-people could they have moved beyond the status of impoverished land-less agrarian laborers. Yet the northern army, in what was perhaps the first major intervention of federal power in a national labor dispute, ensured that both during and after the Civil War the freedmen's dream of landed economic independence would remain an elusive mirage.

VI

This forcible intervention on the side of capital marked a major point of departure for the party of Abraham Lincoln. When the Republicans vaulted to power in 1860, they did so on the basis of a platform that appealed to workingmen's interests, a platform that viewed govern-mental guarantees of access to landownership as the essential prere-quisite for freedom. In fact, Lincoln insisted during the 1860 campaign that access to landownership gave free men their most desirable ave-nue of escape from the repugnant shackles of "wage slavery." For Lincoln, wage slavery meant permanent economic subordination: that is, life as a paid employee working for someone else on someone else's property. It would appear that the Arkansas freedman who asked only for land was reiterating the Republican dogma that saw "Free Soil, Free Labor, and Free Men" as the instrumentalities of the American Dream. When he demanded land, this freedman was throwing the central contradiction of the northern emancipation program squarely in the faces of his so-called liberators.

It may well be that their experience with the agonizing contradic-tions revealed during the war helped to sensitize many conservative Republicans to the ideological inconsistencies that would eventually compel their party to abandon its condemnation of "wage slavery."[96] Although Republicans managed to evade these contradictions during the war by pointing to the prior necessity of saving the Union, the is-sues raised by coming of free labor to the wartime South reemerged during the Reconstruction period. The question of how the federal government would employ its power in disputes between capital and labor grew more and more intense as the American industrial revolu-tion moved forward.

The close interrelation between the suppression of the southern blacks' quest for economic independence and the suppression of the northern workingmen's pursuit of a similar dream makes the study of the wartime origins of southern free labor all the more significant. If Benjamin Quarles accurately assessed the revolutionary transformation of labor relations within the Confederacy when he insisted that blacks had already won de facto freedom prior to Appomattox, our examination of this experience indicates that its extent varied, depending upon local labor systems and the timing of emancipation. Nonetheless, the study of the origins of the southern transition to free labor offers an exciting and potentially fruitful area of inquiry in the study of nineteenth-century southern society. Only by analyzing the specifics of various southern regional economies can scholars uncover the evidence needed to locate the American experience with emancipation in its broadest global context. Situating this experience in a global context will demonstrate its complementarity with the nineteenth-century international transformation that witnessed the successful substitution of capitalist forms of free labor for preexisting systems of unfree agrarian labor.

Notes

1. Harold D. Woodman, "Sequel to Slavery: The New History Views the Postbellum South," *Journal of Southern History* 43 (Nov., 1977): 523.

2. Carl Degler, *Place Over Time: The Continuity of Southern Distinctiveness* (Baton Rouge: Louisiana State Univ. Press, 1977), 75–76.

3. Eugene D. Genovese, *The Political Economy of Slavery: Studies in the Economy and Society of the Slave South* (New York: Pantheon, 1965). Genovese argues for a distinction between concepts of economic *growth* and economic *development*. He contends that the slave economy of the antebellum South grew but did not develop; that is, the slavery economy expanded but the social limitations imposed by slavery prevented capitalist development. For a discussion of the postbellum economy see, Roger L. Ransom and Richard Sutch, *One Kind of Freedom: The Economic Consequences of Emancipation* (New York: Cambridge Univ. Press, 1977), 9–12.

4. Paul M. Gaston, *The New South Creed: A Study in Southern Mythmaking* (New York: Knopf, 1970), 217–46.

5. Woodman, "Sequel to Slavery," 550, 552.

6. Benjamin Quarles, *The Negro in the Civil War* (Boston: Little, Brown, 1969), viii.

7. Bell Irvin Wiley, *Southern Negroes: 1861–1865* (New Haven: Yale Univ. Press, 1938); W. E. B. Du Bois, *Black Reconstruction in America, 1860–1880* (New York: Atheneum, 1969; orig. pub. 1935).

8. Wiley, *Southern Negroes*, 3–23.

9. Du Bois, *Black Reconstruction*, 55–83. For a suggestive refinement of Du Bois's thesis, see Julie Saville, "Freedom vs. Freedom: Views of Emancipation in South Carolina in 1865" (unpublished paper, 1983).

10.   Lewis Cecil Gray, *History of Agriculture in the Southern United States to 1860*, 2 vols. (Washington: Carnegie Institution, 1932), 2:752–78.

11.   Louis S. Gerteis, *From Contraband to Freedman: Federal Policy toward Southern Blacks, 1861–1865* (Westport, Conn.: Greenwood, 1973), 119–33.

12.   Ibid., 193.

13.   James L. Roark, *Masters without Slaves: Southern Planters in the Civil War and Reconstruction* (New York: Norton, 1977), 68–108.

14.   David Montgomery, *Beyond Equality: Labor and the Radical Republicans, 1862–1872*, 2d ed. (Urbana: Univ. of Illinois Press, 1981), vii–xi; C. Vann Woodward, *Origins of the New South, 1877–1913* (Baton Rouge: Louisiana State Univ. Press, 1951), 23–50.

15.   James Ford Rhodes, *History of the Civil War* (New York: Macmillan, 1919), 49–50.

16.   Colonel Tyler to West Virginia Slaveholders, July 4, 1861, cited by George Washington Williams, *A History of the Negro Troops in the War of the Rebellion, 1861–1865* (1888; reprint, New York: Bergman, 1968), 72–73.

17.   General Orders No. 3, Nov. 21, 1861, Hdqtrs, Dept. of the Missouri, Record Group (RG) 393, National Archives (NA).

18.   John Beatty, *Memoirs of a Volunteer, 1861–1863*, ed. Harvey S. Ford (New York: Norton, 1946), 24.

19.   General John C. Frémont, "A Proclamation" Aug. 30, 1861, United States War Department, *The War of the Rebellion: A Compilation of the Official Records of the Union and Confederate Armies*, 128 vols. (Washington, D.C.: Government Printing Office, 1880–1901), 1st ser., 3:466–67 [hereafter cited as OR]; Frémont to Lincoln, Sept. 8, 1861, and Lincoln to Frémont, Sept. 11, 1861, Ibid., 477–78, 495–96.

20.   John D. Inskeep Diary, Oct. 10, 1861, Ohio Historical Society, Columbus, Ohio.

21.   Lew Wallace to Wife, June 8, 1862, Wallace Collection, Indiana Historical Society, Indianapolis, Ind.

22.   Alan Pinkerton, *The Spy of the Rebellion, Being a True History of the Spy System of the United States Army* (New York: G. W. Dillingham, 1883), 194.

23.   John Wilkens to Sister, March 11, 1862, Wilkens Papers, Indiana Historical Society.

24.   Beatty, *Memoirs*, 56. A ledger kept by northern forces near Jackson, Tennessee, records the arrival of 2,100 fugitives. Men under twenty-five account for 54 percent of the total; adding their numbers to those of the men under forty yields a striking 82 percent of the total number of runaways accepted at Jackson prior to January 1, 1863. Men outnumbered women by a ratio of nine to one, and fully 90 percent of the total group of fugitives were under the age of forty.

25.   Entry for Aug. 26, 1862, Mildred Thorne, "The Civil War Diary of Cyrus Boyd," *Iowa Journal of History* 50 (1952): 178.

26.   Emma Lou Thornbough, *The Negro in Indiana Before 1900* (Indianapolis: Indiana Historical Bureau, 1957), 187–88.

27.   Major William Thompson to Wife, Sept. 25, 1861, Edwin C. Bearrs, "Civil War Letters of Major William Thompson," *Annals of Iowa* 38 (1965–67): 440.

28.   Ira Berlin, Joseph P. Reidy, and Leslie S. Rowland, *Freedom: A Documentary History of Emancipation, ser. 2, The Black Military Experience* (New York: Cambridge Univ. Press, 1982), 183–299; Nell Irvin Painter, *Exodusters: Black Migration to Kansas after Reconstruction* (New York: Knopf, 1977).

29.   Gerteis, *From Contraband to Freedman*, 16–17, 71–72.

30.   James McPherson, *The Struggle for Equality: Abolitionists and the Negro in Civil War and Reconstruction* (Princeton: Princeton Univ. Press, 1964), 52–98.

31.   Quarles, *Negro in the Civil War*, 58–61; Gerteis, *From Contraband to Freedman*, 11–19.

32.   James Parton, *General Butler in New Orleans: A History of the Administration of the Department of the Gulf in 1862* (New York: Mason Brothers, 1864), 491.

33.   John W. DeForrest, *A Volunteer's Adventures: A Union Captain's Record of the Civil War*, ed. James H. Crushore (New Haven: Yale Univ. Press, 1946), 17.

34.   Frank Harding to father, May 3, 1862, in Robert C. Reinders, "A Wisconsin Soldier Reports from New Orleans," *Louisiana History* 3 (1962): 362–65.

35.   Butler to Stanton, May 25, 1862, Records of the Secretary of War, RG 107, NA.

36.   DeForrest, *A Volunteer's Adventures*, 26–27.

37.   Butler to Phelps, May 28, 1862, Dept. of the Gulf [DG], RG 393, NA.

38.   DeForrest, *A Volunteer's Adventures*, 26–27; Gerteis, *From Contraband to Freedman*, 68–71.

39.   General Orders No. 32, May 27, 1862, DG, RG 393, NA; John W. Phelps Diary, May 27, 1862, New York Public Library.

40.   Butler to Halleck, Sept. 1, 1862, DG, RG 393, NA; Gerteis, *From Contraband to Freedman*, 65–82.

41.   Richard West, *Lincoln's Scapegoat General: A Life of Benjamin Butler, 1819–1893* (Boston: Houghton Mifflin, 1965), 182–83; John D. Winters, *The Civil War in Louisiana* (Baton Rouge: Louisiana State Univ. Press, 1963), 141.

42.   C. Peter Ripley, *Slaves and Freedmen in Civil War Louisiana* (Baton Rouge: Louisiana State Univ. Press, 1976), 40–89.

43.   Ibid., 90–101. See also J. Thomas May, "Continuity and Change in the Labor Program of the Union Army and the Freedmen's Bureau," *Civil War History* 17 (1971): 245–54; William Messner, "Black Violence and White Response in Louisiana, 1862," *Journal of Southern History* 41 (1975): 25–36.

44.   Phelps Diary, May 17, 1862.

45.   Phelps Diary, Aug. 2 and 7, Sept. 1, 1862; Butler to Phelps, Aug. 2, 1862, DG, RG 393, NA.

46.   William Watson, *Life in the Confederate Army: Being the Observations and Experiences of an Alien in the South during the American Civil War* (New York: Scribner & Welford, 1888), 398.

47.   Magnolia Plantation Journal, Sept., 1862–Jan., 1863, Southern Historical Collection [SHC], Chapel Hill, N.C.

48.   Gray, *History of Agriculture*, 2:739–51; J. Carlyle Sitterson, *Sugar Country: The Cane Sugar Industry in the South, 1753–1950* (Lexington: Univ. of Kentucky Press, 1953).

49.   Ransdell to Moore, May 24, 1863, in George P. Whittington, "Concerning the Loyalty of Slaves in North Louisiana in 1863: Letters from John H. Ransdell to Governor Thomas O. Moore Dated 1863," *Louisiana Historical Quarterly* 14 (1931): 491–93.

50.   Ripley, *Slaves and Freedmen*, 77–78.

51.   Mark Schmitz, "The Transformation of the Southern Cane Sugar Sector, 1860–1930," *Agricultural History* 53 (Jan., 1979): 270–85.

52.   Samuel Carter III, *The Final Fortress: The Campaign for Vicksburg, 1862–1863* (New York: St. Martin's, 1980), passim.

53.   Armstead L. Robinson, "Day of Jubilo: Civil War and the Demise of Slavery in

the Mississippi Valley, 1861–1865," (Ph.D. diss., Univ. of Rochester, 1977); V. Jacque Voegeli, *Free but Not Equal: The Midwest and the Negro during the Civil War* (Chicago: Univ. of Chicago Press, 1967), 160–82.

54. Thomas to Stanton, April 1, 1863, Adjutant General's Office, Adjutant General's Letters Sent, RG 94, NA.

55. Senneca B. Thrall to wife, Feb. 25, 1863, in Mildred Thorne, "An Iowa Doctor in Blue: The Letters of Senneca B. Thrall, 1862–1864," *Iowa Journal of History* 58 (1960): 137.

56. C. C. Carpenter to Kate Burkholder, Aug. 29, 1862, in Mildred Thorne, "A Commissary in the Union Army: Letters of C. C. Carpenter," *Iowa Journal of History* 53 (1955): 65.

57. George P. Rawick, *The American Slave: A Composite Autobiography*, 19 vols. (Westport, Conn.: Greenwood, 1972), 6:347.

58. FitzGerald Ross, *Cities and Camps of the Confederate States*, ed. Richard B. Harwell (Urbana: Univ. of Illinois Press, 1958), 120–21.

59. DeForrest, *A Volunteer's Adventures*, 77.

60. Sherman to Parsons, Aug. 30, 1862, District of West Tennessee, RG 393, NA.

61. Selfridge to Porter, Nov. 8, 1862, U.S. Department of the Navy, *Official Records of the Union and Confederate Navies in the War of the Rebellion*, 35 vols. (Washington, D.C.: Government Printing Office, 1894–1920), 1st ser., 23:472.

62. Laura S. Haviland, *A Woman's Life Work* (Chicago: privately published, 1887), 264.

63. John Eaton, *Report of the General Superintendent of Freedmen's Department of the State of Tennessee and State of Arkansas for 1864* (Memphis: n.p., 1865), 8.

64. Janet Sharp Hermann, *The Pursuit of a Dream* (New York: Oxford Univ. Press, 1981), 41–60.

65. John Eaton, *Report of the General Superintendent of Freedmen's Department for the Army of the Tennessee for 1863* (Memphis: n.p., 1864); Eaton, *Report of the General Superintendent for 1864.*

66. "Report of the Superintendent of Freedmen for Arkansas for 1864," OR, 3rd ser., 4:24; Maude Carmichael, "Federal Experiments with Negro Labor on Abandoned Plantations in Arkansas, 1862–1865," *Arkansas Historical Quarterly* 1 (1942): 101–16.

67. John Q. Anderson, "Joseph Carson, Louisiana Confederate Soldier," *Louisiana History* 1 (1969): 48–49.

68. Frank L. Richardson to Mother, Sept. 23, 1861, Richardson Papers, SHC.

69. Edward Burrus to father, Jan. 19, 1863, and Edward Burrus to father, Feb. 21, 1863, Burrus Papers, Louisiana State University (LSU), Baton Rouge, La.

70. Nimrod Porter Diaries, Aug. 16, 1863, SHC.

71. David S. Donelson to General Sneed, June 15, 1861, Pillow Papers, Confederate Army Records, Generals' Papers, RG 67, NA.

72. Harrison Trexler, "The Opposition of Planters to the Employment of Slaves as Laborers by the Confederate Army," *Mississippi Valley Historical Review* 27 (1940): 216; Bernard H. Nelson, "Confederate Slave Impressment Legislation, 1861–1865," *Journal of Negro History* 31 (1946): 403; Wiley, *Southern Negroes*, 124–25.

73. H. E. Sterkx, *Partners in Rebellion: Alabama Women in the Civil War* (Rutherford, N.J.: Fairleigh Dickinson Univ. Press, 1970), 133.

74. Bell Irvin Wiley, *Plain People of the Confederacy* (Baton Rouge: Louisiana State Univ. Press, 1943), 78.

75. Mary B. Eskeridge to Wm. Woodruff, Nov. 20, 1862, in Ted R. Worley, "At

Home in Confederate Arkansas: Letters to and from Pulaski Countians, 1861–1865," *Pulaski County Historical Society Bulletin* 2 (1955).

76. Mary Cheatham to Mattie Ready, Sept. 12, 1862, Morgan Papers, SHC.

77. Anonymous Natchez Diary, Nov. 15, 1863, Mississippi Department of Archives and History (MDAH), Jackson, Miss.

78. Judge Robert S. Hudson to Col. Spira, April 20, 1863, MDAH.

79. Samuel Andrew Agnew Diaries, July 28, 1862, SHC.

80. G. W. Humphreys to Governor John Pettus, Dec. 16, 1862, Governor's Papers, MDAH.

81. Sylvester Fairchild to wife, Aug. 7–10, 1862, Fairchild Papers, Indiana Historical Society.

82. Harold D. Woodman, "Post Civil War Southern Agriculture and the Law," *Agricultural History* 53 (Jan., 1979): 319.

83. Amelia Mandeville to Rebecca Mandeville, Jan. 17, 1864, Mandeville Family Papers, LSU.

84. Susanna Clay to Clement C. Clay, Sept. 5, 1863, Clay Family Papers, Duke University Library, Durham, N.C. See also Ruth Ketering Nuermberger, *The Clays of Alabama: A Planter-Lawyer-Political Family* (Lexington: Univ. of Kentucky Press, 1958), passim.

85. "An Act to Prevent Slaves from exercising pretended ownership over property," Texas General and Special Laws, 10th Legislature, called session, 1864, May 26, 1864.

86. Sarah Garrett to Governor Clark, Sept., 1864, Governors' Papers, MDAH.

87. Judge Robert S. Hudson to Governor Clark, Oct. 6, 1864, ibid.

88. District Attorney G. C. Chandler to Governor Clark, Jan. 16, 1865, ibid.

89. *Brothers vs State 2 Coldwell 201*, in Helen Catterall, ed., *Judicial Cases Concerning American Slavery and the Negro* 5 vols. (Washington, D.C.: Carnegie Institution, 1926–37), 2:580.

90. *Arkansas True Democrat*, July 8, 1863, cited by Michael B. Dougan, "Life in Confederate Arkansas," *Arkansas Historical Quarterly* 31 (1972): 33.

91. Wiley, *Plain People*, 88.

92. Anna Affleck to Mrs. Perry, Nov. 20, 1864, Perry Papers, University of Texas Library, Austin, Texas.

93. Agnew Diary, June 1, 1865, SHC.

94. Alexander Pugh Diary, Jan. 18, 1865, Pugh Family Papers, LSU.

95. Edward Magdol, *A Right to the Land: Essays on the Freedmen's Community* (Westport, Conn.: Greenwood, 1977), 141.

96. Montgomery, *Beyond Equality*, 335–86.

THAVOLIA GLYMPH

Freedpeople and Ex-Masters: Shaping a New Order in the Postbellum South, 1865–1868

WHEN the Civil War began, few Americans would have predicted its revolutionary outcome. North and South, most Americans would have found some common ground of understanding in the assessment of a contemporary that "the South fought to sustain slavery, and the North fought not to have it hurt."[1] By the time President Lincoln issued the Emancipation Proclamation, however, abolitionist Wendell Phillips could write smugly and victoriously that the proclamation "floated into a dead issue."[2] Phillips exaggerated but little. The "loss of mastery" which historian James Roark has so finely detailed began long before Robert E. Lee surrendered, and Jefferson Davis correctly labeled it "a break in time."[3] In the aftermath of war, however, planters wanted to forget that the rupture had ever occurred and moved to promote a reconstruction that would dam the revolutionary flood released by the emancipation of their slaves and their political and military defeat. But if former masters remained unconvinced of their decisive defeat, their former slaves, singularly transformed by the events of war and emancipation, determined to assure their former masters of the fundamentally changed circumstances that Davis's dictum implied. The adoption of the share-wage system in the postbellum South set the stage for the ensuing struggle.

While freedom for most slaves was secured only with the final military victory of the northern armies, the years of war had dealt a crushing blow to the old order, and the actions of the slaves had contributed to its collapse. Almost immediately after the commencement of hostilities, slaves throughout the South began to move—as if singlemindedly—to aid in the transformation of a war for union into a war for freedom. Their actions soon forced a reassessment and revision of purpose, goals, and strategies by both Union and Confederate forces, as they signally adjusted agendas by refusing to stay "in their place." Throughout the South they abandoned slavery, defying the faith of the Confederacy in their loyalty and that of northerners—the Lincoln administration in particular—in their patience. National and state legislatures, Confederate and Union, became as much battlegrounds as Gettysburg or Vicksburg; fugitive slaves commanded the attention that neither side wanted to give them. Their flight contested the will even of Union commanders who believed that the war had nothing to do with slavery or freedom and eventually prompted the passage of legislation affirming the slaves' sensibilities about the basic nature of the war.[4] Affirming their sensibilities about the nature of freedom became the next item of contention.

With juridical freedom secured, but land ownership blocked, the former slaves fought to assert their definition of freedom, opposing that avowed by their former masters—including the less than inspired wisdom of those who agreed with a former South Carolina Sea Island planter that "no man ought to pay a negro more than 10 cents for a day's work"—and that of northern advocates of a South reconstructed with free labor in the production of staple crops.[5] In fact, long before the old order crumbled in the ruins of war, the "great question" concerned the transformation of the South to a free labor economy. In the South Carolina lowcountry, for example, wartime efforts to resume staple crop production met resistance from blacks who opposed a reorganization of their lives and labor which meant planting cotton. They preferred, instead, to plant subsistence crops, and even when finally persuaded that they must plant cotton, they refused to do so by gang labor, breaking up into smaller groupings—usually by family—to work separate parcels of land in what one observer labeled "a most republican spirit."[6] Northern observers were as mystified by this behavior as lowcountry blacks were by the directive of a Union naval officer to "plant cotton and thus to become of use to themselves."[7] In similar ways, the transition to a free-labor system in the postbellum South pitted former masters against former slaves in a struggle over the meaning of freedom itself, and pitted sometimes one or the other, or both, against the emerging and often competing notions of freedom in the northern states.[8]

New and old circumstances shaped the terms of the battle and thus the "free-labor system that emerged. Former slaveholders throughout the South clung tenaciously to the legacy of power associated with their centuries-long tenure as owners of both land and labor and to the ideology which had been shaped by and which confirmed that experience. "The people of this state," reported the assistant commissioner of Mississippi for the Bureau of Refugees, Freedmen, and Abandoned Lands, "boast that when they get Freedmen affairs in their own hands, the negroes, to use their expression, 'will catch hell.'"[9] Indeed, some of the initial responses of the former masters parallel those of the French bourgeoisie of the sixteenth century, to whom the peasant revolts appeared as a "heinous conspiracy . . . which would literally turn the world upside down and confound the meaning of words and the sense of things." The nobles, magistrates, and bourgeoisie of France, in the words of one scholar, "credited the crowd of artisans and peasants with a horrible desire to kill them all, if not eat them, on the day of Mardi Gras in order to marry their wives and divide up their property."[10] When the Civil War ended, southern whites voiced similar fears of social inversion, and rumors of black insurrections dotted the columns of southern newspapers. For the French bourgeoisie, the day of reckoning was to be Mardi Gras; southern whites feared Christmas of 1865.

During the Civil War, slaves had collaborated in the defeat of their masters, but they had not initiated the war that freed them. As the battle lines over the meaning of freedom became clearer, southern whites feared that the failure of blacks to gain land and to win other concessions that would give substance to their definition of freedom would produce a major insurrection—and this time it would be initiated by the blacks.[11] For the former masters, that day of reckoning never came. Their land was not confiscated, their former slaves did not demand restitution from them or retake up arms against them, and they were not forced to grind their faces in the sweat of toil. But whether they recognized it or not, their world had already been transformed. Indeed, their owned changed status made them symbols of the fact, and the most notable symbol was not far distant, the freed slaves.

In addition to the loss of billions of dollars in property, former masters faced the seemingly contradictory—to some, even preposterous—notion of having to bargain with laborers who were not only free persons but also their former slaves, and within a new set of political relations as well. The circumstances were at once discrete and inseparably linked. Most crucial was that the social relations of production had become vastly different. As C. Vann Woodward writes, "After the curtain fell on the old South, the same cast had to be taught strange new roles and learn new lines."[12] For the former masters, another scholar notes, "the bright, satisfying world of masters and slaves had given way to the dull, disquieting reality of employers and employees, of landlords and tenants."[13] Indeed, the new reality was difficult and disquieting, but seldom dull.

The majority of the former slaves too lacked tutelage in the workings of a free labor economy. But, as one bureau agent reported, "they certainly know all about slavery and have no idea of returning to any such condition."[14] For both the ex-slaves and the ex-masters, the transition proved uneven, painful, frustrating, and chaotic as planters grappled with their loss of privileged access to property and authority and the freedpeople challenged their former masters' determined efforts to reconstitute the old order. Nowhere was the challenge more engaging than over the control of labor, as it was in every post-emancipation plantation society.[15] That contest informed all others.

The efforts to resume staple crop production on the prewar scale placed planters in the uncomfortable position of employers but without the advantage of their northern bourgeois counterparts, who had "developed in the womb of industry and the towns."[16] It was, nevertheless, a position they clearly preferred to that of becoming landlords. Former masters hoped to rebuild their fortunes and prestige along the distinct and established route of the past, or, at the least, with as few detours as possible. And since, for the most part, land was not made available to the freedpeople, their customary place in the southern economy and society seemed established. "The citizens of this state," reported the Freedmen's Bureau assistant commissioner of Mississippi, "will not rent land or sell to Freedmen. They say, if the freedmen are allowed land, they will not hire out for wages. . . . The whites know that if the negro is not allowed to acquire property or become a landowner he must return to the plantation and work for wages that will barely support himself and family; and they feel this kind of slavery to be better than none at all."[17] Yet whatever the desires of former masters—and ultimately those of former slaves as well—the northern military victory and the emancipation of the slaves represented, in part, the triumph of the industrial revolution's claim to slavery's ultimate demise, and thus of free labor ideology.[18]

Northerners spoke of organizing the South "anew," by which they meant transforming its social relations of production. And that, to some, was a relatively simple matter. As one contemporary expressed it, "It is not men we have to fight, it is the state of society that produces them."[19] That verdict soon changed, but at first northern planters, missionaries, teachers, and bureau agents eagerly took up the challenge. It quickly became clear, however, that the men and the state of society which had produced them were one unfathomable whole. From the beginning, the free labor system that emerged in the South was a peculiar adaptation of the northern variant; if nothing else, the legacy of slavery ensured that it would be.

Of course, there was more. The majority of the freedpeople did not become landowners, but just as continuity between the past and present collided with the fact of emancipation, so too did the northern free labor ideology collide with the freedpeople's desire for autonomy—even where land was not made available. The share-wage system which emerged in the immediate postwar years thus became the focus of the conflict over labor control.

The share-wage system arose primarily, as several scholars have pointed out, because many planters lacked the resources to pay cash wages, because the disruption of the credit institutions during the war had dismantled the familiar means of financing planting operations, and because the former slaves, for reasons that remain indistinct in most historical accounts, preferred it. For planters, the use of what one historian terms "retained wages" offered certain other distinct advantages.[20] From the planters' point of view, the share-wage system not only resolved the cash-shortage problem but also, perhaps more importantly, provided the means of access to black labor least suggestive of change in the nature of the antebellum plantation system. Planters believed it would, at the same time, encourage greater industry from the former slaves by giving them an interest in the output. The freedpeople would continue to work and live as before, receiving their compensation at the end of the year in shares of the crop, and the plantation store would become an effective substitute for the old smoke house.[21]

To the freedpeople, however, the adoption of the share-wage system was suggestive of radical change in the reorganization of the plantation and in the reorganization of their lives. The freedpeople not only expressed a preference for share wages over cash wages when they had the option to choose, but also often demanded them even when offered no options. Bureau agents acknowledged that the "system proved very attractive to the freedmen." They failed, though, to appreciate why it did, attributing the freedpeople's preference for share wages over "moderate wages paid at stated periods," as one agent put it, to "the indistinct prospect of some great gain in the future."[22]

The freedpeople disagreed with that assessment. From their perspective, the share-wage system offered the discrete prospect of immediate gain; it meant to blacks that they were partners with the landowners in the enterprise of planting, harvesting, and marketing the crop, and that meant the opportunity for independence and control over the disposition of their labor power. The acknowledged disadvantages associated with the uncertainty of the return failed to outweigh these factors.[23] The more the freedpeople pressed their interpretation of the new order, the more planters came to regret what now seemed clearly to have been an overly hasty appraisal of the benefits of adopting the share-wage system. As one bureau agent reported:

> The freedman claims under such contracts frequently that he has no other work to do but to cultivate and gather the crop, that being a partner in the concern he ought to be allowed to exercise his own judgment in the management of the plantation, that he ought to be able to lose time, when it suits his convenience to do so and when according to his judgment his labor is not needed in the field, that he ought to have a voice in the matter of gathering the corn and cotton and in the ginning, packing and selling of the latter product—while the employer claims that the labor of the employee belongs to him for the whole year. . . . that he must have the sole and exclusive management of the plantation and that the freedman must obey his orders.[24]

As partners in the undertaking of making a crop, blacks demanded a voice in the management of the plantation and the right to order their lives as they believed best—just as the planters did. In other words, the former slaves sought the opposite of everything that eventually came to be associated with the system of share wages and what later came to be called sharecropping.

Wherever the share-wage system occurred in the postbellum cotton South, the freedpeople's insistence upon their interpretation of the relations of production under the system rested on notions of freedom and the ownership of their labor power that were at variance with the ideas of their former masters and often equally galling to the northern advocates of a new South. The former slaves' contention that share wages implied an interest in plantation management was particularly disturbing since it challenged the theories of labor-management relations coming to dominance, though not uncontested, in industrializing nations, where alienation from the means of production and subjection to the demands of the marketplace increasingly defined the emerging order. In important ways, therefore, northerners were no better equipped for the task of transforming the former slaves into a working class than southerners.[25] Planters who resisted adoption of the share-wage system clearly understood, in their own way, the danger in the freedpeople's interpretation. Planters in Hinds County, Mississippi, for instance, vehemently opposed the efforts of blacks to become semi-independent tenants, pledging not to rent to them or to accept them as croppers unless they came under the planters' complete control.[26] Their view was shared by the South Carolina planter and former master who emphatically maintained: "As soon would I think the Lowell manufacturer should share his manufactured calico with his operatives as to approve giving my labour part of the crop."[27]

When bureau agents complained that planters understood "as little of the nature of their obligations to the freedmen—as the freedmen do to the planters,"[28] they were expressing, as well, how little they, too, understood the freedpeople's preference for share wages, or, to put it differently, how well they understood how fundamentally the former slaves' struggle challenged the basic tenet of the ideology that they in fact represented. The freedpeople's insistence on share wages thus understandably perplexed the agents of the Freedmen's Bureau as much as it sometimes did the former masters, and probably more. Equipped with the language of free labor ideology but not the capacity to mold it to southern peculiarities, local agents bombarded their superiors with letters testifying to their inability to comprehend the freedpeople's "druthers." Oftentimes their superiors were no less confounded. When Maj. Gen. Alvan C. Gillem took over as assistant commissioner of the Freedmen's Bureau in Mississippi, he criticized the prevalent practice of share wages under which the laborers considered "themselves entitled to a voice in the method of cultivation."[29] Indeed, the struggle of the former slaves to enlarge the meaning of freedom caused some observers of the labor problem to conclude, in the words of one northern soldier, that "the negroes appear to have imbibed some very dangerous and fallacious doctrine in regard to when 'Freedom Come!'"[30] To the agents of the Freedmen's Bureau, the freedpeople's notions concerning the implications of working for a share of the crop, however explained, hindered the bureau's task to aid in the transformation of southern society.

Agents of the Freedmen's Bureau generally opposed the share-wage system, preferring that where possible, blacks contract for cash wages. As justification they cited the greater pecuniary rewards of cash wages, the greater certainty of the cash nexus, and the diminished opportunities for fraud on the part of landowners. In so doing, they evinced a lack of understanding of the freedpeople's motives. Major Gillem, for example, supported the system of cash wages "for the same reasons that the poor man seeks the protection of insurance companies whilst the millionaire takes his own risks." It was equally clear to Gillem that the grounds for many of the complaints of both workers and employers that flooded the bureau's offices would fade once the system was abandoned. As disturbing to bureau agents as to former masters was, as Gillem complained, the disposition of the former slaves "to work or play just when so inclined, as in the cases where they are working for shares, for under the latter system, the freedmen are apt to think that they have the right to work or play just as they see fit,"[31] notions plainly menacing to the establishment of a free labor ideology that stressed discipline, punctuality, and obedience to the demands of the market economy. But as Harold D. Woodman has emphasized, while the desire for a docile and easily managed work force was not a concept alien to northern factory owners, the extent of submission demanded of the freedpeople became distinctively southern.[32]

When the freedpeople insisted on share wages, they insisted on a degree of autonomy not only in the planting and marketing of the crop, but in all other areas of their lives as well. Control of family labor was as much a part of their view of the new order as resistance to the performance of tasks not directly tied to the making of a crop or for which they received no compensation, causing former masters to conclude that freedom had had a pernicious result: "an unexpected desire in the blacks to go to themselves." It had, this planter complained, "rendered our black population hitherto so loyal to us, now disposed to consult strangers and the happy influence we once possessed with them is now almost entirely lost, or but slightly appreciated."[33] Clearly, the former slaves' resolute efforts to claim the fruits of their labor and to determine its disposition extirpated what remained of planter repose.

Facing the loss of that "happy influence," the disconsolate planters reacted in kind. Moving to demonstrate that they could easily dispense with southern black labor altogether, they attempted to attract and experimented with immigrant and northern black labor. Castigating these efforts in a letter to Major General O. O. Howard, commissioner of the Freedmen's Bureau, Samuel Thomas stated, in undisguised contempt: "The Southern white men, true to their instincts and training are going to Mexico or Brazil, and talk of importing Coolies—Irishmen—anything, to avoid work; anyway to avoid putting their shoulders to the wheel." In language clearly derisive in its tone, he suggested that former masters "attend to their own affairs, and make arrangements for the working of the disbanded rebel army, in the cornfields and the workshops." He added: "There are today as many houseless, homeless, poor wandering, idle white men in the South as there are negroes, yet no arrangements are made for their working."[34] In the end, of course, despite notions and schemes to replace black laborers with immigrants, the plantation labor force remained predominantly black and southern-born, and other efforts by planters to reorganize their world ended in equally dismal failure.

At first, southern planters viewed coercion as a still viable means of restoring a world they initially believed not irreparably lost. The Mississippi Apprenticeship Act of 1865, for example, established the right of civil officials to apprentice all blacks under the age of eighteen who were "orphans" or whose parents could not or would not support them. The state's vagrant law, amended in 1865, not only made unemployment a crime but also made unlawful certain assemblies and any association between blacks and whites on terms of equality. In addition, the act levied a tax of one dollar on all blacks for the support of the indigent, making failure to pay "*prima facia* evidence of vagrancy." The 1865 Act to Confer Civil Rights made it illegal for blacks to rent or own land or houses outside of incorporated towns or cities. Finally, and perhaps to forestall the anticipated Christmas Day massacre, the Mississippi legislature forbade blacks to carry firearms or knives or to make seditious speeches or insulting gestures; it also penalized cruelty to animals. Inability to pay the fines would find blacks on the auction block to be hired out "at public outcry."[35]

Such laws obviously placed obstacles in the path of the creation of a black yeomanry, but they did more. They allowed, for example, former masters to apprentice, as orphans, their former slaves on the weakest of evidence as to the family's ability to support children or other relatives; in fact, apprenticeship laws gave former masters priority in access to the labor of those former slaves classified as orphans.[36] Commanding the northern district of Mississippi in December of 1865, Maj. Gen. Manning F. Force observed that the "ruling conviction of the state," was "that the freedmen constitute an element which they [southern whites] call 'the labor of the state,' an element which is valuable when under the absolute control of the employer, and which upon any other condition, would be mischievous."[37] As one former master stated unequivocally, any system whereby the freedman believes "he becomes a partner and has a right to be consulted" is "wrong policy."[38] Such laws also offered some redress to planters like R. S. Adams, who complained that his laborers did as they pleased and even insulted him. These were not, Adams reasoned, "trivial offenses" but "grievous ones."[39] Without doubt, the black codes were also pointedly aimed at disarming the former black soldiers whose enlistment on the side of the Union had helped seal the planters' defeat, and the extreme southern white resentment towards the former soldiers reflected that fact. As Willie Lee Rose explains in her incisive manner, "The black soldier had indeed rejected the past both manor and master in the most conclusive way—by abandoning one and fighting the other."[40]

Mississippi's black codes, like those of other southern states, reflected, chiefly, planters' attempts to resolve the problem of making the transition from mastery to management, a task for which they were fundamentally ill-prepared. When Congress invalidated their best efforts, they often turned in desperation to the Freedmen's Bureau, whose very existence was yet another symbol of their defeat. Bureau agents stood ready and willing to aid and even compel the transformation of former slaves and former masters into new classes. As one agent confidently stated, and with perhaps a bit of arrogance, "time and the Freedmen's Bureau" would ultimately cure any defects in southern whites or blacks that stood in the way of reorganizing southern society in a manner consistent with the principles of free labor ideology.[41] Although some planters found comforting reassurance from local agents who viewed the behavior of the former slaves as the main obstacle blocking the South's transformation, and aided in securing and disciplining the labor force, the opposite was often the case. Samuel Thomas, for example, wrote: "I feel that we are in honor bound to secure to the helpless people we have liberated a republican form of government, and that we betray our trust when we hand these freedmen over to their old masters to be persecuted, and forced to live and work according to the peculiarly southern ideas."[42] But with no other viable recourse, planters such as A. B. Sturdivant were forced to turn to the bureau's agents regardless of the agents' political persuasion. Sturdivant forwarded a group of his laborers to the bureau's local office in order that the agent might "give them a talk." When they returned without having seen the agent, he wrote to the bureau, pleading that the officer let him "know what to do."[43]

After the passage of the Civil Rights Bill of 1866, management problems seem to have become even more acute. Although the black codes had proved ineffective in ordering the transition from slavery to freedom that the planters sought, they had—at least in the minds of the planters—provided some semblance of order and continuity. The invalidation of the codes by the new federal legislation destroyed this source of direction and support, and the number of planters seeking advice increased. "Since the passage of the Civil Rights Bill," one planter lamented, "we do not know how to act." S. H. Harris had neglected to incorporate rules against disrespectful conduct into his contract with the former slaves, and the freedmen, he complained, swore "like our army in Flanders." Even more disconcerting was their reply, when Harris reprimanded them, that their language was outside the terms of the contract.[44]

However, planters who turned to the bureau agents for assistance often found the solutions proffered less than helpful and, at times, incomprehensible. Seeking advice, J. T. Bell stated matter-of-factly, "I am in trouble and will be pleased to have information." The reply from the bureau agent could hardly have been reassuring. If the freedpeople refused to do their jobs according to contract, replied Major John J. Knox, Bell should discharge them, as any northern factory owner would: "Tell her she don't suit you." He added: "It is unnecessary for me to tell you that time or usuage has passed away and you are expected to deal with them as Freemen and Freewomen."[45] Bell was probably mystified by this answer, which merely restated his problem.

Even when planters began to grasp, at least in part, the language of free labor ideology, the basic premises continued to elude them. According to John Greaves, the freedpeople on his plantation in Hinds County, Mississippi, refused to be managed. In exasperation, Greaves wrote, "I am unable to carry on the planting business any longer!" From the bureau he sought a guarantee of "systematic labour," and a "file of soldiers" to maintain order. "The operatives," he continued, "must be under subjection and move in the discharge of orders as promptly & efficiently as the Soldiers in a successful campaign." In the meantime, he wrote, the planters were "broke and dispirited" and had no further use for blacks, who had become an "encumbrance to the country and will drag it down to degradation and Ruin—unless you [the Freedmen's Bureau] who have the power will come to the Rescue!! You can make them work!" Like other former masters, Greaves was merely admitting—although in a convoluted fashion—his inability to manage free labor and simultaneously (perhaps unwittingly) acknowledging what was believed to be northern expertise in this area. Greaves ended his letter in a fit of agitation: "Git me a Tenant—start a *Government* farm on my place! Suggest something that will help me & the poor negroes."[46]

The former slaves continued to press their advantage under the share-wage system, and their former masters groped for answers, resorting, almost always, in the final analysis, to old solutions and worn language. "The negroes," grumbled one former master, "work when they please, do not work on Saturdays at all, get paid for just what they do and rely largely upon hunting and fishing to make up for what they lose in the field." He went on: "Labor must be commanded completely, or the production of the cotton crop must be abandoned." Another planter, J. E. Newman voiced similar complaints when some of his laborers used their free time to visit a nearby town. "The tramps are taken every Sabbath," he griped. Both planters attempted to impress upon the bureau agents the necessity of lecturing the freedpeople on the need for more industry and resurrected the by now hackneyed threat to displace black labor. "If *free black labor* can not be made more industrious tractable and profitable," Joseph Pope concluded, "let us know at once in order that it may be made to yield its position to *free white labor*."[47] The freedpeople, wrote another planter in disgust, "want 10 cents—for each time they water a horse."[48] Most offensive to the planters, however, was not that the freedpeople were less industrious than during slavery but instead that they reserved a portion of their labor power for their sole benefit. After plowing, York, a Mississippi freedman, refused to measure corn and sent word to the planter that he "was going to pull his ground peas off [the] vines."[49]

Planters sometimes found local bureau agents and military authorities sympathetic to their efforts to exercise unlimited control over the former slaves—by force, if necessary—or through the approval of contracts stipulating the forfeiture of wages if workers, for example, left the plantation at night, even after completing their work.[50] The freedpeople, however, continued to resist all such efforts and, at least through 1867, to see the share-wage system as in their best interests. If the complaints of planters provide any indication, they were partly successful. Increasingly typical was the situation on the Belle-Air Plantation in Greenville, Mississippi, as contracting for the 1867 crop got underway. William Bolton's hands had received cash wages for the 1866 crop but demanded a change for the coming year. "My hands proposed to work for me this year i e [*sic*] 1867," he wrote, "under the old overseer if I wd give them an interest in the crop, they to pay for their Clothing & Food, & every thing else, beyond what is on the place to be charged, 1/2 to each party, they are to have an equal interest in the Cotton, Corn & Potatoes grown upon the place."[51]

In the end, however, the attempt by the former slaves to escape white supervision, and to claim some control over their lives and the disposition of their labor under the share-wage system, failed. Planters fought back, circumscribing access not only to the means of production but to subsistence as well.[52] They continued to claim the labor of entire families even when only one member was under contract, using this tactic even as a means to defraud the laborers of any claim to the crop. For example, after securing the freedman's copy of a contract under false pretenses, the planter W. T. Smith informed the freedman that he would receive nothing for his labor, assigning as the reason that the freedman's wife had not worked in the field despite the fact that the contract made no mention of her.[53]

Complaints of fraud had become more numerous by 1867, as "excuses of various kinds were advanced by some debtors with whom the freedmen worked for shares, that nothing was made and accounts were presented showing that the freedmen were in their employers' debt, and in these cases they were held as bound to contract for the coming year for the purpose of liquidating the indebtedness."[54] Abuses such as these prompted the issuance of orders to bureau agents to ensure that where blacks worked for a share of the crop, their portions were delivered to them on the plantations to prevent planters from claiming excessive charges for transportation and commission on sales. General Orders No. 19 of the Fourth Military District of Mississippi, for instance, directed officers to arrest for trial before a military commission any planters accused of attempting to commit such fraud and to prevent the removal of crops before the laborers' share had been determined. Only by this means, wrote assistant commissioner Gillem, would "the laborer become the absolute possessor of the fruits of his toil."[55]

Such problems demoralized the freedpeople, particularly as it became increasingly clear that working for share wages offered no more room for autonomy, or the specific kind of freedom that they sought, than did cash wages, making even more glaring their economic losses. After the various charges for bagging, freighting, and the planter's commission for disposing of the crop had been deducted, the freedpeople often came away with the view that they had been cheated by their employers, as was frequently enough the case.[56] And in cases in which they perhaps were not cheated—in which their educational handicaps placed them at a disadvantage—impressions to the contrary were often sufficient enough to convince them that they were.[57] Yet, even had the former slaves been proficient in arithmetic, they would still have had difficulty comprehending the calculations of some planters. John J. Horne, who had contracted to pay the freedpeople on his plantation one-tenth of the crop, calculated their share of the corn in four cribs in a manner that promised to frustrate even the most astute and learned. "First I multiply the length breadth and depth [of the corn cribs] together," he explained, "then I divide the product by 5 and deduct the Quotient from the Amt [sic]. I then divide the remainder arising from this by 2 as I think one half cob & the other half corn. The Quotient arising from this is the amount of corn in the crib." Horne's laborers did not care much for his division and therefore took what they believed to be their rightful share.[58] Even the matter of what constituted a share became a subject of contention, prompting the following response from an obviously riled plantation superintendent whose hands had taken their complaints to the local bureau agent. "The freedmen," he explained somewhat impatiently to the bureau agent, who had hinted at the possibility of fraud in the contracts, "are to have *half of what* they make. One hand is to get *half* of what *one hand makes*— that which he makes, of course, is considered a *share*; but what the share *will be time* alone *can tell.*"[59] Exasperated bureau agents threw up their hands, Maj. Gen. John J. Knox reportedly declaring, "No man can understand what *constitutes a share!*"[60] To a large extent, of course, the short crop of 1866 and the depressed market of 1867 contributed to the problems facing black and white southerners, compromising the ability of both to make the transition to free labor on their own terms. That the former slaves did not get all they wished should not obscure the fact that their struggle prevented the former masters from getting all they wished as well.

The advantages that former masters had initially seen in adopting the share-wage system faded. Their former slaves had indeed shown an interest in the crop, but not in the manner that planters had in mind. Thus, planters, too, became increasingly disenchanted with the system of share wages. In addition, the codes and penalties for "enticing" and "vagrancy," and the attempts to organize cartels had all failed to have a significant impact on the upward pressure on wages.[61] Planters in the older South were hit especially hard as they attempted to compete with the more fertile western lands. Consequently, discontent seems to have mounted faster in the older regions. Most prominent throughout the South, however, was planter dissatisfaction with their inability to restore the familiar means of control over the laborers.[62] The precipitous decline in cotton prices in 1867 compounded these problems. Planters found it more and more difficult to meet their commitments, and some began decreasing the shares due their laborers,[63] while others went further still. A group of Mississippi planters attempted to use the occasion of economic distress to combine in reducing wages. In the future, others insisted, planters would provide subsistence only, a position advocated in the Vicksburg *Times*:

> It may as well be understood, first and last, that no such price [as five dollars] will be paid. . . . To grow cotton for sale or export, he [the freedman] must compete with the cheapest labor in the world. He must compete with

laborers who do not receive as much per year as negroes demand for a
month of shifless [sic] idleness. If negroes expect to live, they must work in
order that they may live. If they expect to escape the pangs of hunger, they
must make up their minds to work for a subsistence only. The day of high
wages for agricultural laborers, has past [sic], and will return no more. The
negro, who secures food, quarters and fuel, hereafter, as a reward for good
honest, reliable labor, may esteem himself fortunate. . . . There will be no
more riotous living, no more insolent idleness, no impudent vagabond-
ism. . . . The time has come when Sambo and Dinah will be happy to receive the wages paid to the native producers in India, Egypt and China—
when they will be glad to labor for the pittance paid to English colliers! The
day of philanthropy is drawing to a close, and instead of arming their brats,
of both sexes, with a book and a slate, for the schoolroom, they will be
compelled to arm them with the plow and the hoe, wherewith they shall
dig from the earth, the bread they now consume in idleness and harlotry.
The day of flaunting in finery has gone by, to return no more— Instead of
sporting a stovepipe hat, gloves and cane, Sambo must content himself
with the axe and plow, and Miss Dinah instead of flourishing in hoopskirts
and high-heeled boots—instead of flaunting sun-shades and fancy hats and
feathers, will be content to take up a hoe and go to work, as in the good old
days when they had masters and mistresses, and never thought of "being
ladies" and "keeping house."[64]

The majority of southern whites may have applauded such a resound-
ing call to reclaim the fruits of black labor—even with its errors in the
historical account—but most understood clearly enough that those
days would not return.

By the end of 1867, both planters and the freedpeople were ready
to try new arrangements, though for neither had the ultimate goal
changed. The former slaves still sought autonomy, and their former
masters still sought complete control. But once more, in some instances, circumstances outside the control of either led to the adoption
of modes of production not completely satisfactory to either. The result
was that some blacks began to gain access to small sections of land, in
return for which they paid the landowner a share of the crop, thereby
becoming, in a technical sense, tenant farmers.[65] Bureau agents quickly
took note and faithfully recorded this transition from share wages to
sharecropping. In his annual report to Commissioner Howard, Assistant Commissioner Alvan Gillem noted:

In former reports I have remarked that the "share system" has prevailed.
More extended information as to contracts between planters and freedmen
suggests a modification of this statement. As the beginning of the present

year, many of the owners of plantations were discouraged at the hopeless results of the two previous years; they were without means and had exhausted their credit with the merchants who usually furnished them with plantation supplies.—Unable thus to cultivate their own plantations and in order to prevent the lands becoming a burden upon them in the way of taxes, they have made contracts, (in the character of leases) whereby the owner was entitled to a certain amount of Cotton or Corn or a stipulated amt. of money. In these cases the freedmen generally relied on their own resources to procure supplies and not on the credit of the planter with his merchant or factor.

Gillem went on to note that the adoption of the new system had resulted in improvements in settlements with planters and a decrease in the number of complaints made to the Bureau:

The principal Evils of the "share system,"—the ignorance of the freedman of the real nature of the contract,—his uncertainty as to the remuneration which he might receive for his labor,—his reliance on his Employers for all the necessities of life,—his ignorance of the value of supplies,—and his inability to keep accounts and also to understand the unfortunate results of the year's operations even when he was fairly dealt with,—and the power of the employer to defraud him by unjust and complicated accounts,—all these evils were generally corrected by the system of leasing referred to.[66]

Most planters, however, were unwilling to give in to an arrangement which would grant blacks a degree of freedom that many still deemed unspeakable. In the end, those black sharecroppers who became tenant farmers discovered, as did their white counterparts, that the crop liens that merchants and landlords required to ensure payment of rent and loans advanced to produce the crop circumscribed their independence. Few indeed was the number of freedmen who found themselves in a position to rent land with no outside assistance, which soldiers' bounties allowed those referred to in Gillem's report to do. And few indeed was the number of blacks who even became tenant farmers. The majority of the former slaves lost their struggle, becoming no more than hired hands and thus as subject to the close supervision of planters as they had been under the share-wage system. In fact, in many respects their subjection was now greater.

Throughout the South, state legislatures defined croppers as laborers receiving their pay in a share of the crop and maintained that the relationship of landlord and tenant obtained only where one party furnished the land and the other the labor and teams or tools. South-

ern court decisions gave judicial sanction to this interpretation, denying any claim on the part of the laborer to any rights of possession in
the crop.[67] The former slaves' insistence that laborers had an interest in
the crop beyond the payment they received at the end of the year was
thus effectively challenged, as typified by the contract between the
freedman Isaac Caldwell and his landlord, W. Y. Holcom. Under the
agreement, Holcom furnished 125 acres and Caldwell the labor, consisting of ten hands. Though this, and the fact that Caldwell was given
complete control over the production of the crop and management of
the hands, suggests a tenant-landlord relationship, it was not so in fact.
Because Holcom supplied the mules, the contract became one legally
of hire, in addition to the stipulation that under its terms Holcom was
to give Caldwell one-fourth of all that was raised. In effect, therefore,
Caldwell was not paying rent by giving the landlord a share of the
crop.[68] Thus, even where contracts appeared, in practice, to suggest a
tenant-landlord relationship, in a legal sense such was not always the
case. That legal distinction allowed Holcom to step in at any point and
take complete managerial control.[69]

In subsequent years, even planters who had experimented with
tenants moved back, when they could, to the use of hired hands or
croppers. Mississippi planters who had in 1867 favored the system of
share wages, in 1871 recommended a system of wages, holding "farming on shares to be false in theory and ruinous in practice."[70] Most
planters complained, as did Alfred Holt Stone, that renting gave too
much latitude to blacks in matters of accounts and handling the crop,
and that the black tenant believed "he should be left free to work [the]
crop when and as he pleases." On the Dunleith Plantation, the problem was solved through the use of contracts that detailed precisely
what was undertaken by each party, reserved to management absolute
control over all plantation matters, and replaced sharecropper tenants
with sharehands. "It is inevitable," Stone concluded, "that there must
always be a large class of Negro tillers of other men's soils."[71] This type
of contract, as Woodman has noted, allowed planters to retain managerial control over the workplace and, ultimately, over nonworking
hours as well,[72] a point Stone readily conceded: "Certainly the relation
of master and slave no longer exists here, but out of it has been evolved
that of patron and retainer. I so designate it because I know of no other
to which it more nearly approaches. It is not one purely of business,

the ordinary relation of landlord and tenant or of employer and employee."[73] Capitalist social relations thus spread over southern agriculture, if in a peculiarly southern way.

In the end, most former slaves and their descendants remained landless and webbed in the cycle of poverty and indebtedness that was also to become uniquely southern. In 1862, Edward L. Pierce had read to the South Carolina lowcountry slaves from the Epistle of St. James verses that would come to seem meaningless in the wake of redemption and the failure of the blacks to fasten their meaning of freedom on southern—and, indeed, northern as well—society. The "precious fruit of the earth," for which they had had "long patience" yet eluded them.[74] Instead, as W. E. B. Du Bois noted, "the slave gradually became a metayer, or tenant on shares, in name, but a laborer with indeterminate wages in fact."[75]

As the South made the transition to a free labor economy, it remained encrusted in poverty, and the legacy of a racially determined slave economy held fast. Southern black laborers came to understand even more fully than wage workers in northern industrialized society that, as Samuel Thomas stated, "Capital does now, and will for some time to come, carry on great enterprises; and a large portion of the human family, both black and white, must labor for this capital at regulated wages, without any direct interest in the result of the enterprise." As for the former slaves specifically, Thomas had written, "the best we can do is, to place his labor on an equal footing with white labor, and neither endow him with a fortune, nor open up his road to jump at once to ease and affluence, That he does not know how to use or enjoy."[76] It was a meaning of freedom and of the ownership of one's labor power that the freedpeople found difficult to digest, and the continued presence of racism combined with intensified political subjection made it all the more unpalatable.

Notes

1.   Wendell Phillips, *Speeches, Lectures, and Letters* (Boston: J. Redpath, 1863), 529.

2.   Ibid., 530.

3.   James L. Roark, *Masters without Slaves: Southern Planters in the Civil War and Reconstruction* (New York: W. W. Norton, 1977); W. E. B. Du Bois, *Black Reconstruction in America: An Essay Toward a History of the Part Which Black Folks Played in the At-*

tempt to Reconstruct Democracy in America, 1860–1880 (New York: Atheneum, 1969; orig. pub., 1935), 54–83; Jefferson Davis to Col. W. M. Browne, July 1, 1871, Jefferson Davis and Family Papers, Mississippi Department of Archives and History (MDAH), Jackson, Miss.

4.   Du Bois, *Black Reconstruction*, 55–126; Louis S. Gerteis, *From Contraband to Freedmen: Federal Policy Towards Southern Blacks, 1861–1865* (Westport, Conn.: Greenwood Press, 1973); see also Ira Berlin, Barbara J. Fields, Thavolia Glymph, Joseph P. Reidy, and Leslie S. Rowland, eds., *Freedom: A Documentary History of Emancipation, 1861–1867*, ser. 1, vol. 1, *The Destruction of Slavery in the American South* (New York: Cambridge Univ. Press, forthcoming).

5.   Testimony of Frederick A. Eustis before the American Freedmen's Inquiry Commission, 1863, filed with O-328, Letters Received, ser. 12, box 1054A, folder 5A, Records of the Adjutant General's Office, 1780s–1917, RG 94, National Archives (NA) [K-80]. Bracketed file numbers refer to copies of records from the National Archives housed at the Freedmen and Southern Society Project, University of Maryland, College Park, Md.

6.   Edward L. Pierce to Hon. S. P. Chase, June 2, 1862, Records of the Treasury Department Civil War Special Agencies, vol. 19, item 166, Port Royal Correspondence, 5th Agency, RG 366, NA [Q-22]; Pierce to Chase, Apr. 1, 1862, vol. 19, item 107, ibid. [Q-13]; E. S. Philbrick to Ned [Edward] Atkinson, Apr. 12, 1862, vol. 19, enclosed with item 154, ibid. [Q-19]. Though he characterized the behavior of the freedpeople as "republican" in spirit, Philbrick was not pleased. Like other northern advocates of free labor ideology, he believed that the success of the lowcountry experiment in freedom depended upon the former slaves demonstrating that they could produce staple crops for the market without the stimulus of the master's lash. That could not be done, however, if the blacks insisted upon working independently, going crabbing when they should be in the fields, or planting corn when they should be planting cotton. To lowcountry blacks, of course, their behavior did not represent anything novel or revolutionary. Before their masters left, they had acted similarly under the task system so widely used in the lowcountry. The only difference—which, in fact, to them was of major consequence—was their opposition to planting cotton, a task too closely associated with their former enslavement. For a discussion of black autonomy in the lowcountry, see Philip D. Morgan, "Black Society in the Lowcountry, 1760–1810," in Ira Berlin and Ronald Hoffman, eds., *Slavery and Freedom in the Age of the American Revolution* (Charlottesville: Univ. Press of Virginia, 1983), 83–141. See also Willie Lee Rose, *Rehearsal for Reconstruction: The Port Royal Experiment* (Indianapolis: Bobbs-Merrill, 1964).

7.   G. S. Godon to Flag Officer S. F. Du Pont, Mar. 30, 1862, enclosed in Flag Officer S. F. Du Pont to Hon. Gideon Welles, Apr. 6, 1862, Letters from Officers Commanding Squadrons, ser. 30, vol. 3, Naval Records Collection of the Office of Naval Records and Library, 1775–1910, South Atlantic Blockading Squadron, RG 45, NA [T-542].

8.   For a discussion of northern free labor ideology and the making of the northern industrial working class, see Eric Foner, *Politics and Ideology in the Age of the Civil War* (New York: Oxford Univ. Press, 1980); Eric Foner, *Free Soil, Free Labor, Free Men: Ideology and the Republican Party before the Civil War* (New York: Oxford Univ. Press, 1970); David Montgomery, *Worker's Control in America: Studies in the History of Work, Technology, and Labor Struggles* (New York: Cambridge Univ. Press, 1979); and Herbert G. Gutman, *Work, Culture, and Society in Industrializing America* (New York: Knopf, 1976).

9.   Col. Samuel Thomas to Maj. Gen. O. O. Howard, Sept. 21, 1865, Records of

the Commissioner, Letters Received, Records of the Bureau of Refugees, Freedmen, and Abandoned Lands (BRFAL), RG 105, NA (Microfilm Publication M826, roll 3, vol. 6).

10.   Emmanuel Le Roy Ladurie, *The Peasants of Languedoc*, trans. John Day (Urbana, Ill.: Univ. of Illinois Press, 1974), 194–95.

11.   Leon F. Litwack, *Been in the Storm So Long: The Aftermath of Slavery* (New York: Knopf, 1979), 295, 425–30.

12.   C. Vann Woodward, "The Southern Ethic in a Puritan World," in *American Counterpoint: Slavery and Racism in the North-South Dialogue* (Boston: Little, Brown, 1971; orig. pub. 1964), 40.

13.   Roark, *Masters without Slaves*, 157.

14.   Thomas to Howard, Sept. 21, 1865, Letters Received, RG 105, NA (Microfilm Publication M826/3/6).

15.   E. J. Hobsbawm, *The Age of Capital, 1848–1875* (New York: Scribner, 1975), 78, 141; Studies which address this conflict in other post-emancipation societies include Eric Foner, *Nothing But Freedom: Emancipation and Its Legacy* (Baton Rouge: Louisiana State Univ. Press, 1983); Thomas Holt, "'An Empire Over the Mind': Emancipation, Race, and Ideology in the British West Indies and the American South," in *Region, Race, and Reconstruction: Essays in Honor of C. Vann Woodward*, ed. J. Morgan Kousser and James M. McPherson, (New York: Oxford Univ. Press, 1982); Frederick Cooper, *From Slaves to Squatters: Plantation Labor and Agriculture in Zanzibar and Coastal Kenya, 1890–1925* (New Haven: Yale Univ. Press, 1980); Rebecca J. Scott, "Gradual Abolition and the Dynamics of Slave Emancipation in Cuba, 1868–86," *Hispanic American Historical Review* 63 (August 1983): 449–97; and Sidney Mintz, *Caribbean Transformations* (Chicago: Aldine, 1974).

16.   V. I. Lenin, "Capitalism in Agriculture," in *Collected Works*, vol. 4 (Moscow: Foreign Language Pub. House, 1960), 113.

17.   Thomas to Howard, Sept. 12, 1865, RG 105, NA, (Microfilm Publication M826/3/6).

18.   Hobsbawm, *The Age of Capital, 1848–1875*, 141–43, 185–87.

19.   Phillips, *Speeches, Letters, and Lectures*, 547.

20.   Historical treatment of the share-wage system has been minimal, consisting, for the major part, of casual and widely scattered remarks. In part this has been the result of confusion over the nature of the share-wage system and its evolution as sharecropping and in part the result of census record-keeping. The origin of the share-wage system in the postbellum South as a compromise between former masters and former slaves is generally recognized, but the nature of the ensuing struggle, once the system was in place, seems less clearly defined. Understanding that struggle helps to place in perspective conflicts which otherwise appear as disjointed, unrelated events. And it helps to shift the focus of attention away from an emphasis on the restoration of circulating credit as the major explanation for the demise of the share-wage system. This essay pays particular attention to the transformation in Mississippi as it relates to the share-wage system. Studies which discuss the share-wage system, with varying degrees of emphasis and interpretation, include, among many others, Litwack, *Been in the Storm So Long*; Roger L. Ransom and Richard Sutch, *One Kind of Freedom: The Economic Consequences of Emancipation* (Cambridge: Cambridge Univ. Press, 1977); Michael Wayne, *The Reshaping of Plantation Society: The Natchez District, 1860–1880* (Baton Rouge: Louisiana State Univ. Press, 1983); Jonathan M. Weiner, *Social Origins of the New South: Alabama, 1865–1885* (Baton Rouge: Louisiana State Univ. Press, 1978); Peter Kolchin, *First*

Freedom: The Responses of Alabama's Blacks to Emancipation and Reconstruction (Westport, Conn.: Greenwood Press, 1972); and Vernon Lane Wharton, *The Negro in Mississippi, 1865–1890* (New York: Harper and Row, 1947).

21.   Lawrence N. Powell notes that northern planters viewed plantation stores as a key ingredient in the establishment of free labor ideology on southern ground. They believed that the material rewards dispensed by these plantation stores could effectively replace the lash in inciting the freedpeople to disciplined and industrious labor (Lawrence Powell, *New Masters: Northern Planters during the Civil War and Reconstruction* [New Haven: Yale Univ. Press, 1980], 87–93).

22.   Contracts filed with the Freedmen's Bureau for the Western District of Mississippi in the fall of 1865, for example, reveal an overwhelming preference on the part of the freedpeople for share wages. For the month of October, twenty contracts embracing 355 hands were filed; 255 of these laborers chose share wages. The following month, eight additional contracts were filed with the same pattern evident: only 20 of the 265 laborers involved opted for cash wages. Lt. Winslow S. Myers to Capt. J. H. Weber, October 1865, Records of the Assistant Commissioners, Letters Received, ser. 2347, RG 105, NA; Myers to Weber, Nov. 26, 1865, ibid.; Capt. Z. B. Chatfield to Maj. Geo. D. Reynolds, Dec. 31, 1865, Records of the Assistant Commissioners, Unregistered Letters Received, ser. 2268, RG 105, NA.

23.   I have discussed this in "Wages, Sharewages, Sharecropping: The Transition from Slavery to Freedom" (paper delivered at the annual meeting of the Association for the Study of Afro-American Life and History, Chicago, Ill., 1976). See also Ransom and Sutch, *One Kind of Freedom*, 94–99.

24.   As quoted in Lawanda Cox and John H. Cox, eds., *Reconstruction: The Negro and the New South* (Columbia: Univ. of South Carolina Press, 1973), 341.

25.   For a discussion of some of the problems encountered by northern planters, particularly their inability to transfer, in whole, northern free labor ideology, see Powell, *New Masters*, 74–75, 97–122, and passim; Rose, *Rehearsal for Freedom*, 326–69.

26.   Wharton, *The Negro in Mississippi*, 64.

27.   As quoted in Eric Foner, "Reconstruction and the Crisis of Free Labor," in *Politics and Ideology*, 118–19.

28.   Lt. L. C. Hubbard to Lt. Col. R. S. Donaldson, Aug. 5, 1865, Letters Received, ser. 2188, box 4, RG 105, NA [A-9304].

29.   Maj. Gen. Alvan C. Gillem to Maj. Gen. O. O. Howard, Oct. 10, 1867, Records of the Commissioner, Letters Received, RG 105, NA (Microfilm Publication M826/3/6, fr. 14).

30.   Capt. Henry A. Shorey to Genl. E. B. Fillebrown, July 9, 1865, Records of the U.S. Army Continental Commands, 1821–1920, Miscellaneous Letters Received, ser. 4171, Dept. of the South, RG 363 Pt. 1, NA [C-1468].

31.   Gillem to Howard, Oct. 10, 1867, RG 105, NA (Microfilm Publication M826/3/6/13).

32.   Lt. O. B. Foster to Capt. J. H. Weber, Nov. 30, 1865, Records of the Assistant Commissioners, Letters Received, ser. 2347, RG 105, NA. On this point, see also Harold D. Woodman, "Sequel to Slavery: The New History Views the Postbellum South," *Journal of Southern History* 43 (Nov., 1977): 549–50, 554; Montgomery, *Workers' Control in America*, 3–4, 90.

33.   Capt. E. B. Heyward to Genl. D. E. Sickles, Dec. 13, 1865, Records of the United States Army Continental Commands, 1821–1920, Letters Received, ser. 4109, Dept. of the South, RG 393, Pt. 1, NA [C-1383].

34. Thomas to Howard, Sept. 21, 1865, RG 105, NA (Microfilm Publication M826); Powell, *New Masters*, 73–74.

35. Edward McPherson, *The Political History of the United States during the Period of Reconstruction, April 15, 1865–July 15, 1870* (New York: Da Capo Press, 1972; orig. pub. 1871), 29–32.

36. See, for example, W. A. Thomas to J. J. Knox, Feb. 16, 1866, Unregistered Letters Received, ser. 2250, RG 105, NA [A-9224].

37. Maj. Gen. M. F. Force to Maj. M. P. Bestow, Dec. 13, 1865, Letters and Telegrams Sent, vol. 31/49, ser. 2150, Dept. of No. Dist. Miss., RG 363, Pt. 2, NA [C-2128].

38. As quoted in Foner, *Nothing but Freedom*, 45.

39. R. S. Adams to Chaplain of the Freedmen's Bureau, Scooba Station, Miss., Sept. 27, 1865, Miscellaneous Records, box 46, ser. 2260, RG 105, NA [A-9427].

40. Willie Lee Rose, "Masters without Slaves," in Willie Lee Rose, *Slavery and Freedom*, ed. William W. Freehling (Oxford: Oxford Univ. Press, 1982), 84.

41. Meyers to Weber, Oct., 1865, Letters Received, ser. 2347, RG 105, NA; See also Whitelaw Reid, *After the War: A Tour of the Southern States, 1865–1866* (New York: Harper and Row, 1965; orig. pub. 1866), 431 and passim.

42. Thomas to Howard, Sept. 21, 1865, RG 105, NA (Microfilm Publication M826).

43. A. B. Sturdivant to Capt. Bennett, Nov. 8, 1865, Unregistered Letters Received, ser. 2137, RG 105, NA.

44. S. H. Harris, to Maj. Ga. S. Smith, May 30, 1866, Letters Received, ser. 2136, RG 105, NA.

45. J. T. Ball to Maj. J. J. Knox, [Mar., 1866], Unregistered Letters Received, ser. 2250, RG 105, NA; Brvt. Maj. Jno. J. Knox to Mr. Jno. T. Ball, Mar. 20, 1866, Unregistered Letters Received, ser. 2250, RG 105, NA.

46. Jno. M. Greaves to Maj. S. S. Sumner, Dec. 25, 1867, Unregistered Letters Received, ser. 2201, box 43, RG 105, NA [A-9366].

47. Jos. Danl. Pope to Maj. Gen. Q. A. Gillmore, June 29, 1865, Miscellaneous Records, ser. 4171, Dept. of the South, RG 393, Pt. 1, NA [A-9416]; J. E. Newman to Maj. J. J. Knox, June 11, 1866, Letters Received, ser. 2249, box 46, RG 105, NA [A-9416]; Newman to Knox, May 15, 1866, ibid.

48. Wm. F. Robert to Gen. Q. A. Gillmore, Aug. 4, 1866, Records of the Army Headquarters, Letters Received, ser. 22, box 100, vol. 85, RG 108, NA [S-15]. Similar complaints can be found in other accounts. See, for instance, Powell, *New Masters*, 103.

49. Sturdivant to Bennett, Nov. 8, 1865, Unregistered Letters Received, ser. 2137, RG 105, NA.

50. Hubbard to Donaldson, Aug. 5, 1865, Letters Received, ser. 2188, box 4, RG 105, NA [A-9304].

51. William H. Bolton to Maj. Gen. Wood, Dec. 9, 1866, Letters Received, ser. 2052, box 4, RG 105, NA [A-9093].

52. See Steven Hahn, "Common Right and Commonwealth: The Stock Law Struggle and the Roots of Southern Populism," in *Region, Race, and Reconstruction*, ed. Kousser and McPherson, 56.

53. John G. Walden to Lieut. F. T. Cunningham, Sept. 15, 1867, Letters Received, RG 105, NA (Microfilm Publication W32, roll 22).

54. Gillem to Howard, Oct. 10, 1867, RG 105, NA (Microfilm Publication M826/10–11).

55. Ibid.

56. Contract between J. F. Winchester and C. Prince and 55 Freedmen [1866], Miscellaneous Records, ser. 1021, box 30, RG 105, NA [A-5790]; A. W. Mitchell to Maj. G. D. Reynolds, Jan. 16, 1866, Letters Received, ser. 2268, box 47, RG 105, NA [A-9467].

57. For example, see Litwack, *Been in the Storm So Long*, 422.

58. John W. Horne to Maj. G. D. Knox, Feb. 21, 1866, Unregistered Letters Received, ser. 2250, box 46, RG 105, NA [A-9425].

59. Bvt. Maj. Jno. J. Knox to J. D. Hardy, Apr. 21, 1866, Letters Received, ser. 2246, vol. 199, RG 105, NA; Hardy to Knox, Apr. 12, 1866, Letters Received, ser. 2249, RG 105, NA.

60. Hardy to Knox, Apr. 12, 1866, ibid.

61. Joseph D. Reid, Jr., "Sharecropping as an Understandable Market Response: The Post-Bellum South," *Journal of Economic History* 33 (March, 1973): 110; Wharton, *The Negro in Mississippi*, 62–64.

62. Fred A. Shannon, *The Farmer's Last Frontier: Agriculture, 1860–1897* (Toronto: Farrar & Rinehart, 1945), 85–88; Oscar Zeichner, "The Transition from Slave to Free Agricultural Labor in the Southern States," *Agricultural History* 13 (Jan., 1939): 24–25, 29–30.

63. Peter Kolchin, *First Freedom*, 43–44; Wharton, *The Negro in Mississippi*, 69.

64. Article enclosed in J. P. Bardwell to Rev. J. R. Shepherd, Jan. 2, 1866, Commissioner's Reports, RG 105, NA. Also enclosed is Assistant Commissioner Alvan C. Gillem's General Orders No. 23 supporting this move on the part of planters. The order directed commanding officers to "notify the leading colored men & take any other such measures as may be necessary to give general publicity of the fact that all freedmen will be required to earn their support during the coming year & go to work upon the best terms that can be procured; even should it furnish a support only." Anyone disobeying the order was to be arrested as a vagrant.

65. Lieut. Geo. W. Carliss to Lieut. Stuart Eldridge, Apr. 9, 1866, Letters Received, ser. 2052, RG 105, NA; R. H. Nesbit to Col. B. F. Smith, Apr. 20, 1866, Records of U.S. Army Continental Commands, Letters Received, ser. 2392, box 1, Dept. of the South, RG 393, NA [C-1609]; Joel Williamson, *After Slavery: The Negro in South Carolina during Reconstruction, 1861–1867* (Chapel Hill: Univ. of North Carolina Press, 1965), 126.

66. Gillem to Howard, Dec. 12, 1868, RG 105, NA (Microfilm Publication M826/7/122–25).

67. Harold D. Woodman, "Post–Civil War Southern Agriculture and the Law," *Agricultural History* 53 (Jan., 1979): 326–29.

68. Contract between W. Y. Halcom and Isaac Caldwell, freedman, Jan. 14, 1867, Contracts, ser. 216, box 38, RG 105, NA.

69. Woodman, "Post–Civil War Southern Agriculture," 337; Arthur Raper, *Preface to Peasantry: A Tale of Two Black Belt Counties* (New York: Atheneum, 1968; orig. pub., 1936), 149; U.S. Dept. of Agriculture Joint Investigation, "Yazoo Segment: Mississippi Backwater Areas Study—Land Tenure Section," 1942, Records of the Bureau of Agricultural Economics: Division of Farm Management and Costs, Reports, Speeches, and Articles Relating to Farm Management, RG 83, NA.

70. Wharton, *The Negro in Mississippi*, 63.

71. Alfred Holt Stone, "The Negro in the Yazoo-Mississippi Delta," in *Studies in the American Race Problem* (New York: Doubleday, Page, 1908), 110, 115–17, 130–36.

72. Wharton, *The Negro in Mississippi*, 69.

73. Stone, "The Negro in the Yazoo-Mississippi Delta," 91.

74. "The Negro at Port Royal," report of E. L. Pierce, Government Agent, to the Hon. Salmon P. Chase, Secretary of the Treasury, (Boston, 1862), pp. 11, 13, University of Texas Library, Austin, Texas. This passage was one of several which Pierce read to the lowcountry blacks.

75.   W. E. B. Du Bois, "Of the Quest of the Golden Fleece," in *The Southern Common People: Studies in Nineteenth Century Social History*, ed. Edward Magdol and Jon Wakelyn (Westport, Conn.: Greenwood Press, 1980), 259; R. Pearce, "Sharecropping: Towards a Marxist View," *Journal of Peasant Studies* (Jan.–Apr., 1983): 42–70.

76.   "Report of Col. Samuel Thomas, Provost Marshal, &c," in *Extracts from Reports of Superintendents of Freedmen*, comp. Rev. Joseph Warren, (Vicksburg, Miss.: Freedmen Press Print, 1864), ser. 1, 32.

BARBARA JEANNE FIELDS

The Advent of Capitalist Agriculture:
The New South in a Bourgeois World

SITTING one afternoon on the gallery near the open window of Will
Varner's store and talking rather louder than was strictly necessary,
William Faulkner's unforgettable itinerant sewing machine salesman,
the ubiquitous V. K. Ratliff, laid out for his fellow loungers the difference between the Yankee and the southern way of doing things:

> If a fellow in this country was to set up a goat-ranch, he would do it purely
> and simply because he had too many goats already. He would just declare
> his roof or his front porch or his parlor or wherever it was he couldn't keep
> the goats out of a goat-ranch and let it go at that. But a Northerner dont do
> it that way. When he does something, he does it with a organised syndicate
> and a book of rules and a gold-filled diploma from the Secretary of State at
> Jackson saying for all men to know by these presents, greeting, that them
> twenty thousand goats or whatever it is, is goats. He dont start off with
> goats or a piece of land either. He starts off with a piece of paper and a
> pencil and measures it all down setting in the library—so many goats to so
> many acres and so much fence to hold them. Then he writes off to Jackson
> and gets his diploma for that much land and fence and goats and he buys
> the land first so he can have something to build the fence on, and he builds
> the fence around it so nothing cant get outen it, and then he goes out to
> buy some things not to get outen the fence.

Ratliff regarded the Yankee would-be capitalist from the same
sardonic and indulgent distance from which he contemplated all the
world's vanity and vexation of spirit. Nevertheless, for all his bemused
detachment, Ratliff himself became an agent of that Yankee's "pro-jeck,"
the middleman twice removed who rounded up the last fifty goats required to prevent the goat ranch from becoming "a insolvency." In the
process he gave a fillip (as if any were needed) to the career of the new-
est local aspiring capitalist, Flem Snopes. He did all this, it is true, in
furtherance of his own inimitable brand of closely reasoned and tightly
plotted skulduggery. That is why he positioned himself by the open

window of the store and spoke in tones that could not help being over-heard inside. But the Yankee's agent, and Snopes's, he became all the same. Even had he not set himself on the trail of "that passel of goats of Uncle Ben Quick's," he was still an agent of Yankee capitalism within his four-county circuit. As a seller of sewing machines—and apparently a persuasive one—he was an efficient local agent of mass-market capitalism. And though the wholesaler from whom he acquired his machines had offices in Memphis, it would be remarkable indeed if the factory that produced the machines lay anywhere south of Mason and Dixon's line. Some years later Ratliff entered the wholesale grocery business with Wallstreet Panic Snopes, whose firm, by the time it had become the largest of its kind in north Mississippi, would no doubt have been "a organised syndicate" with "a book of rules and a gold-filled diploma from the Secretary of State at Jackson."[1]

An acute and ironic observer of the world about him, Ratliff—standing in for Faulkner himself—no doubt fully appreciated the perversity and contrariety of affairs by which the keen-eyed critic became a party to the capitalist transformation of the South as much as the grossest New South loudmouth, the staunchest devotee of moonlight and magnolias, and the most wretched and confused pawn of events. The historian must appreciate it also, for that was the predicament of the postbellum South. After the epochmaking upheaval of the Civil War and Reconstruction, a prolonged period of transition set in—prolonged, but neither random nor arbitrary. The abolition of property rights in man removed the most important obstacle to the consolidation of capitalist agriculture in the South (and, eventually, the consolidation of capitalist industry as well). That imposed a definite direction upon the ensuing period of transition, for all the hybrid characteristics that have led some people to the mistaken conclusion that nothing fundamental changed at all. Amid the apparently kaleidoscopic movement of the fragments of prewar southern society, a clearly definable process was underway, to which the unwitting and unwilling contributed as surely as the witting and the willing.

That process was the emergence and growing dominance of bourgeois capitalist social relations, and it had been underway for centuries on a world scale. Feudal society in western Europe enjoyed its classic period from the eleventh century to the early fourteenth. Thereafter it entered a decline that even renewed expansion between the mid-fifteenth and mid-seventeenth centuries could not mask. Beneath the surface of royal absolutism, lineal heir of feudalism, the remnants of feudal sovereignty steadily decomposed. By the late eighteenth century, the lingering political emblems of feudal privilege in western Europe concealed an agrarian world whose typical cultivator was a peasant free in fact if not at law; and a commercial world which, though still mercantile rather than industrial, generated enough social energy to force even the most firmly rooted absolutist regimes to come to terms with it.

England led the way. There, notwithstanding the temporary survival of a good many cottagers and smallholders of various sorts, the peasantry had all but disappeared by the mid-eighteenth century. The durable features of the countryside were the landholding nobility and gentry, a small class of capitalist tenant farmers, and a rural majority who lived by performing agricultural labor in exchange for wages. Herein lies the essence of capitalist social relations in agriculture. Those who work the land are not the property of the landowner, like chattel slaves, nor are they compelled by law to work for the landowner, like serfs or villeins. Instead, they are the owners of their own persons, which they may not sell, and of their ability to work (their labor power), which they may sell in exchange for the necessaries of life. At the same time, those who work the land do not receive the necessaries of life from masters (as slaves often did), nor do they independently own land, tools, and other means of labor and subsistence (as free peasants and even most serfs did). For this reason they not only *may* sell their labor power—because they own it and it is therefore theirs to sell; but they *must* sell their labor power—because they own nothing else, and therefore can acquire the necessaries of life only by working for a wage.

In no other country had capitalist social relations conquered the field to the extent that they had in England by the late eighteenth century. But the very strength of the English, reflected especially in their success at the tribal warfare in which the European monarchies incessantly engaged, forced the other states of western Europe to compete with the English on their own ground. The efforts of absolute monarchs to strengthen their regimes for this contest confirmed and reinforced the power of the rising bourgeoisie. Capitalism thus made its influence felt far beyond the area where capitalist social relations had come to predominate.[2]

Perverse and contrary as are most human affairs, the advance of capitalism was neither smooth nor even. From time to time it engendered its own opposite, creating backwaters that emphasized the main flow chiefly by their failure to participate directly in it. As capitalist social relations advanced in western Europe, the economic complex of which they constituted the most dynamic part drew to itself a vast hinterland in which noncapitalist relations of coerced labor were reinforced, extended, or—where necessary—created from scratch. Part of this hinterland lay in the colonies, including those of the Americas, which provided certain key agricultural and mining raw materials. Another part lay in eastern Europe, where the reduction of the peasantry to a new and crushing serfdom from the sixteenth century on eventually provided the means of supplying western Europe with the agricultural commodities, especially grains, that were essential for its growing and increasingly urban population.[3] Thus, even as slavery, serfdom, and other forms of servile labor declined over western Europe, there arose powerful landed upper classes in both the New World and the Old who claimed personal sovereignty over slaves and serfs. At times these classes derived some color of sanction from the history of a land and people to which they themselves belonged. At other times (in the Americas, for example) they were as frankly exotic as the colonial outposts whose hereditary rulers they sought to become.

In due season the river reclaimed its channel, flooding the backwaters and tributaries that its own meandering course had created, incorporating these once more into the main flow. The combined force of the French Revolution and the industrial revolution—the dual revolution, a noted historian has called them—set that flood in motion. Itself an expression of advancing bourgeois social relations, the dual revolution became the most potent means of their further advance. The economic repercussions of the industrial revolution combined with the political repercussions of the French Revolution to impart a purposeful direction to subsequent world history. In western Europe the superannuated husks of feudal society fell away, doomed as surely by the struggle to resist as by the struggle to extend the influence of the French Revolution. That Revolution also (for a time, anyway) abolished slavery in France's New World colonies—an example Britain eventually followed in the Caribbean, as did the independence movements that liberated much of mainland Spanish America from Spain. The final extraordinary outburst of the revolutionary era, the failed revolutions of 1848, did away with serfdom in central Europe, and reabolished slavery in the French Caribbean.[4]

To other areas the change came more slowly, but just as surely. In the United States slavery at first took new heart from the dual revolution. Rearrangement of colonial empires (as, for example, when Napoleon decided to sell Louisiana) gave slavery a vast territory in which to expand, while the insatiable appetite of English factories for cotton supplied the best of motives for expansion. Among its many accomplishments, the American Revolution won independence for what was to become the world's most powerful class of slaveholders. But the spectacular expansion of American slavery was a supernova, a star exploding brilliantly on the eve of its death. For the dual revolution fed simultaneously the expansion of the slave states and of their chief rival, the free states, while preparing the moment when their rivalry would erupt in a war that slavery could not hope to survive. Slaveholders in Cuba and Brazil carried on for two more decades after their North American counterparts, though not just as before, and by 1888 slavery had been abolished in both countries. In Russia and eastern Europe and in the Dutch colonies of the Americas, the formal liquidation of serfdom occurred almost simultaneously with the death agony of slavery in the United States.[5]

Capitalist social relations, in short, were on the march on a world scale, lending unity to widely scattered events that superficially appeared each to follow its own idiosyncratic logic. Begin where they might and travel what route they would, these events ended as part of the process—worldwide in scope—that wrenched labor power, land, instruments of labor, and means of subsistence out of the realm of personal dominion, communal obligation, and hereditary right and made them commodities—the individual private property of their owners— freely alienable on the market. The rhythm of the world capitalist economy established the backdrop for this process in individual countries. The period from 1848 to 1873 was one of heady expansion, which gave its tone to the vast social changes that followed the defeat of the revolutions of 1848. The period from 1874 to 1893 was a time of economic distress, spawning the first incontrovertibly worldwide depression of the capitalist era.[6] Capitalist relations emerging during this period took on the color of their grim backdrop. Placing the American South in its world context means recognizing the unity of a historical drama enacted worldwide, with each local performance couched in the vernacular of the local audience.

The local performance of this drama enacted in the vernacular of the American South occurred in consequence of a war of national consolidation whose cost in blood and treasure had no peer in the developed world of its day. In that contest a landed, slaveowning class had to fight to the death. There could be no ultimate compromise between the sovereignty of a bourgeois nation-state and the sovereignty of master over slave. Nothing more remarkably demonstrates the truth of this statement than the fate of slavery in the loyal slave states (Maryland, Kentucky, Missouri, and Delaware). Though the administration of Abraham Lincoln did all it could to protect the slave property of the loyal citizens of those states, the war doomed slavery there as surely as in the Confederacy.

An illustration from Maryland may stand in for hundreds of comparable episodes that cumulatively made nonsense of any effort to preserve the sovereignty of slaveowners while asserting the sovereignty of the nation-state by military means. In August, 1864, Annie Davis, a slave in Bel Air, Maryland, had a difference of opinion with her mistress, who refused to let her visit relatives on the Eastern Shore. Slavery remained legal in Maryland, since the Emancipation Proclamation of January 1, 1863, applied neither to loyal states nor to certain portions of rebellious states under federal occupation. But three years of war had taught Annie Davis that a power closer than Heaven outranked her mistress, and the knowledge corroded her mistress's authority. When denied her wish, Annie Davis took her case to higher authority, writing to Lincoln: "Mr. president   It is my Desire to be free. to go to see my people on the eastern shore. my mistress wont let me   you will please let me know if we are free. and what i can do. I write to you for advice. please send me word this week. or as soon as possible and oblidge.   Annie Davis." For Annie Davis, the sovereignty of her owner had suffered irreparable damage, even though neither the army, the law, nor the President could offer the slightest comfort for her disobedience.[7]

Not only was the sovereignty of master over slave what the struggle was fundamentally about, but the collaboration of the slaves proved essential to carrying that struggle forward. The Union could not secure its goal of national unification except by enlisting (in both the military and the everyday senses of the word) the help of the slaves. Brig. Gen. John W. Phelps showed his grasp of the situation during his memorable contest of wills with Maj. Gen. Benjamin F. Butler in the summer of 1862 over the arming of slaves. Justifying his plan to turn slaves into an army of liberation, Phelps explained: "A small class of owners . . . stand between [the slaves] and their Government, destroying its sovereignty. . . . If it cannot protect all its subjects, it can protect none, either white or black."[8] Republican politicians, the political agents of the struggle for national unification, learned the lesson more slowly than General Phelps, but they learned nevertheless. They put slaves into the confiscation acts, into the March, 1862, article of war, into the army, into the Emancipation Proclamation—everywhere, in short, that the exigencies of the war itself taught them they must. Even the Confederate government eventually realized that it could not defeat the Yankees while according privileged status to the sovereignty of master over slave. The interference of Confederate officers who impressed slaves into service as military laborers played no small part in undermining the authority of owners, even in areas untouched by the Union army. By the end of the war, the Confederacy was prepared to offer freedom to slaves who would fight on its behalf. Only Appomattox forestalled the playing out of this final absurdity.

The combination of these two circumstances—a fight over competing forms of sovereignty and the involvement of the slaves—gave a radical cast to the Union's triumph. Not only was some three billion dollars in private property abolished without compensation, but the freedmen acquired full citizenship and, in time, the right to vote.[9] The old aristocracy, stripped of the economic foundation of its dominance (namely, ownership of slaves in large numbers)[10] lost for a crucial period its power within the national government. It returned as a junior partner, to find that important decisions had been taken while its back was turned. Former large slaveholders even had to surrender temporarily their control at the state and local level. Though the freedmen and their Republican allies could not hold onto power for long, the damage to the old order proved irreversible. The planters were not shot, exiled, or made to work for wages picking cotton or driving spikes on the transcontinental railroad. But they lost their old means of extracting the agricultural surplus product. However fondly they might have wished to reestablish slavery, or a reasonable facsimile, they could not; the freedmen, backed by the federal government and not least by the Freedmen's Bureau, would not permit it. If the planters wished to make a comeback, they must do so within a new set of social and political relations, by that very act transforming themselves into a new and capitalist class and sealing more securely the doom of the old order.

Some historians doubt nevertheless that anything very profound changed as a result of the Civil War. When all is said and done, they argue, the antebellum planters were powerful not because they owned slaves but because they owned land. The war deprived them of their slaves but not of their land; therefore, the war cannot have occasioned a profound social change.[11] That conclusion is open to question on a number of counts. Many planters held onto their land only by so burdening it with debt as to surrender effective control to whoever put up the money. Moreover, planters who managed to hold their land until 1870—when most studies of the question stop short—may well have lost it thereafter. With the onset of depression in the 1870s, planters faced a disastrous combination of indebtedness, falling commodity prices and land values, and the constant battle to subdue the strong-willed freedmen. W. E. B. Du Bois has left a remarkable eyewitness account, dating from the 1890s, of plantations in Georgia's black belt abandoned because their owners could not master that combination of adverse circumstances.[12]

Furthermore, any evaluation of the post–Civil War South that rests on the supposed continuity of landed property must take into account differences between regions within the South: between old cotton or rice areas and new ones, between capital-intensive sugar production and labor-intensive cotton production, and so on. The reconstruction of the sugar economy, with central factories and intensified mechanization, seems to have entailed a substantial influx of newcomers and outside capital. When the rice industry, moribund in the Carolina and Georgia lowcountry, was born again on the Louisiana Gulf Coast, it was through the agency of outside capital and entirely new personnel. The new cotton empire of the Yazoo-Mississippi delta involved both external capital and a new planter class, whether or not the planters concerned thought of themselves as such.[13]

More important than any of these questions of empirical detail, however, is the false premise upon which the entire argument rests: namely, that ownership of land rather than ownership of slaves formed the basis of the planters' power as a class. If landownership alone conferred wealth and power, slavery would have been unnecessary on the huge American continent. Precisely because land was abundant and fairly cheap, forcible methods were required to make large numbers of people work the land for someone else's benefit. Without such methods, land was worthless. That expressive old phrase "land-poor" accurately describes the predicament of many a plantation family that ended up with land and little more. Even economists have confirmed this fact, though camouflaging it in their peculiarly inanimate language: labor, they say, was the main economic "constraint" in antebellum American agriculture.[14] The abolition of slavery revolutionized the social relations of the old plantations, even where it made no discernible change in the personnel.

Nor is that all. The abolition of slavery revolutionized more than relations between former masters and former slaves. The hardy independence of the backcountry white yeomanry—snug and secure in fastnesses where its own notions of property, market, family, community, and right had room to grow—was as much a product of slavery as was the dependence of the slaves. Had an up-and-coming bourgeoisie instead of the slaveholding planters been the fulcrum of antebellum southern society, the yeomen would have become what so many of their northern counterparts became: the home market of capitalist industry and its rural auxiliary. Industrial capitalism—in the guise of roads, canals, and railroads; cities with their hungry (and non-food-producing) populations; intensive cultivation and labor-saving agricultural technology; and a whole apparatus of land promoters and speculators—left few areas of the rural North immune to its imperious demands. But the social, economic, and political predominance of the large slaveholders preserved, at least for a time, the immunity of the southern yeomen. They could live in largely self-sufficient communities, trading in local markets and subordinating production of cash crops to the needs of general farming. Once the planters had been obliged to concede that the forms, at least, of electoral democracy belonged to all white men regardless of estate, they were content not to bother the yeomen as long as the yeomen did not bother them.[15]

The signs of trouble that appeared even before the war may have played their part in making the heart-stopping gamble of secession look like the safest bet. The pressure of population growth invested the yeoman economy with an expansionist urge to match that of slavery. Heads of families wishing to bequeath to all their children farms of sufficient size to ensure independence increasingly needed larger holdings in order to do so. Rising land values during the 1850s made it harder and harder to meet this need, inducing some yeomen to plunge heavily, though temporarily, in the cash-crop economy. Rising hire and purchase costs of slaves restricted the alternative of using slave labor in an effort to increase production of a marketable surplus. By the outbreak of the war, some yeoman communities may well have been approaching the limits of the slave system's capacity to satisfy their aspirations.[16] A student of the secession movement in Georgia has concluded that the great planters favored secession from fear that a Republican national administration might use federal patronage to build a free-soil movement in their back yard.[17] The yeomen's communities would have been a shrewd place to drive a wedge—and long experience has shown that federal patronage, skillfully inserted, is no mean wedge.

At all events, the war upset the truce between planters and yeomen, for it required massive interference with the yeomen by the Confederate government. The conscription of men and the seizure of farm produce and livestock undermined the economic foundation of the yeomen's communities, while the infamous "twenty-nigger law" (exempting from conscription one owner or overseer for every twenty— later fifteen—slaves) offered an embarrassing advertisement of the planters' class privilege. Never, as a group, very enthusiastic about secession, some yeomen took to passive and others to armed resistance. Desertion, draft resistance, and fifth-column activity reminded the Confederate regime that it had more to worry about than the Yankees.[18]

Defeat finished what the war began. With slavery abolished and the slaveholders obliged to resort to market methods for compelling the labor of former slaves, the yeomen lost their own buffer against the advance of market relations. The faster these advanced in the plantation belt, the nearer came the day of their penetration into the backcountry. Yeomen attempting to safeguard their independence by gambling on the staple economy, as some had done in the 1850s, became unwitting participants in the destruction of their former way of life. The long depression of the late nineteenth century mopped the floor with smallholders whose prospects for independence hinged on gambling in the world market for cotton or grains. Each defeat at this gamble meant the loss of yet another increment of autonomy and the taking of yet another step toward entire subjection to the social relations of the market.[19]

Not only yeomen but anyone who tried to get a footing in the new terrain by restoring familiar arrangements ended by promoting the dissolution of those arrangements. The antebellum cotton factors moved quickly to reestablish themselves once the dust of war had settled, and for a time succeeded in doing so. But their very success shifted the ground beneath them and, in the end, made them obsolete. The opening of transportation links to the interior posed the threat that growers might bypass factors altogether. To protect themselves, factors entered the business of buying cotton, financing itinerant merchants to act on their behalf. Unfortunately, the better organized this system became, the less need for local buyers to deal with factors at all. Similarly, the factors' efforts to maintain control over the business of providing credit to cotton growers ended by promoting the very competitors who put the factors out of business. Because distant factors could not be sure that growers to whom they advanced credit would in fact send them the cotton at the end of the season, they began dealing with local merchants instead of local growers. As in the buying of cotton, so too in the provision of credit, the merchants eventually outgrew their dependence upon the factors.[20]

Perhaps the most dramatic example of the strength of the inherent tendency toward capitalist social relations is the institution of sharecropping. A product of the clash between freedmen and former slave-owners over the shape of new labor relations, it eventually led both groups in a direction that neither one had foreseen or intended. After being denied their warmest desire—land of their own to farm—the freedmen fought tenaciously over the terms on which they would offer their labor. The results varied. In the Louisiana sugar parishes (for reasons not yet entirely clear but probably having to do with the exclusively plantation scale of sugar production and with the early infusion

of outside capital) wage labor emerged almost immediately. Rice workers in the lowcountry battled their employers to a draw which, compounded by natural calamity, finished off the industry: the new rice
industry of Louisiana was, so to speak, born-again capitalist. In the cotton and tobacco areas, sharecropping was the usual outcome. It began
as a compromise between the planters' wish to restore the work discipline of slave days and the freedmen's desire for independence. It
quickly emerged as a transitional form on the way to capitalist wage
labor, its evolution in that direction faithfully recorded by the southern
legal system.[21]

It is not surprising that the union of these two irreconcilable opposites—the standpoint of the ex-slaves and that of their ex-masters—
produced a hybrid and therefore infertile offspring. In the end, sharecropping stood not as a symbol of the freedmen's triumph but as a measure of their defeat. Instead of a landowning peasantry, they became
the next thing to wage hands. Deprived thus of a foundation for economic independence, they could not ultimately hold onto political
power. The loss of political power, in turn, menaced the freedmen's
small, hard-fought steps toward economic independence. The reason
for their defeat was not that they retained too many of the incidents of
slavery, but rather that they acquired too many (though not all) of the
incidents of proletarian status. On the other hand, sharecropping—
better suited to the labor needs of white smallholders[22]—represented
no shining victory of the planters. Its spread betrayed their weakness,
their inability to carry through the transition to capitalism fully on
their own terms.

It was certainly a peculiar brand of capitalism that slowly came to
life in the South, so peculiar that a number of people deny that the
South was headed toward capitalism at all until World War II. Poverty
and backward agricultural technique, along with coercion of the labor
force through debt peonage, anti-enticement laws, and outright terror,
do not much resemble the "classic capitalism" of industrial England.[23]
But England had the good fortune to be first. No country that followed
had the advantage of a centuries-long period of preparation, with no
serious rivals at the key moment. Subsequent routes to capitalism have
traversed ground irrevocably altered by the English industrial revolution, and by a world market disposing (unlike the feudal one) power
sufficient to determine the internal development of nations falling un-

der its sway. Besides, the English had to use coercive methods themselves, before the "invisible" hand of the market could appear to work
by itself. Those methods ranged from a Tudor law enslaving vagabonds
who absconded from forced labor to the Master and Servant Law of
1823 and the New Poor law of 1834, both designed to enforce the discipline of the marketplace upon reluctant conscripts to the proletariat.[24]

Countries arriving at capitalist social relations after England have
not been able to do so in the English way; the English closed off their
route by using it first. Establishing a scheme of classification so widely
influential that many have forgotten its source, V. I. Lenin identified
two historical routes to capitalist agriculture. In one, which he labeled
"American," the free farmer carries through the transition to capitalist
agriculture, in a society "free from all medieval fetters, from serfdom
and feudalism, on the one hand, and from the fetters of private property in land on the other"—land, in this view, being available at nomi-
nal cost from the vast public reserves. In the other, which Lenin called
"Prussian," feudal relations linger on, to be gradually adapted to capitalist forms by the landed upper class itself. In Prussia the landed nobility—the Junkers—did not succumb to bourgeois revolution but
consolidated their social and political domination for decades after the
revolution of 1848.[25]

Obviously, this schema calls for numerous qualifications, especially
as regards what we now know were considerable "fetters of private
property" intervening between the American public domain and its
final settlers, who were very far from acquiring the land free of charge.
Furthermore, close examination of northern farming communities has
shown that the free farmer did not universally or automatically take to
capitalist commercial production.[26] Of more importance to the matter
at hand, however, is the fact that the persistence of landed property in
the postbellum South has persuaded some people that the American
south followed the "Prussian road" to capitalist agriculture, led by a
planter class that preserved its power intact even after losing the Civil
War. That interpretation calls for scrutiny.

In the original Prussian way, the Junkers not only held landed
property; they also dominated the machinery of the national state,
with the weak bourgeoisie playing a subaltern role. In the United
States the opposite held true. The American bourgeoisie was not weak.
It was the most autonomous, if not indeed the most powerful, part of

the coalition that had defeated the Confederacy, and it grew more powerful in the course of the conflict. The 1877 settlement that formally ended Reconstruction—which is what Barrington Moore, Jr., had in mind when he referred to a Prussian alliance in the United States—reflected the weakness not of the bourgeoisie, but of the old Southern planter class.[27]

A brief comparison of the authentic Prussian way with what took place in the American South clearly shows a world of difference. In Prussia itself, in the Hapsburg Empire (especially in Austria and Bohemia, but in Hungary as well), in Russian Poland, and (though to a lesser extent) in Rumania, landowners were not only able to hold on to the lion's share of landed property and limit the political rights that accompanied emancipation, but they were also able, using their decisive political and economic weight, to tailor to their advantage the transition to capitalist relations. The Prussian landowners received massive assistance as well in the form of large cessions of land or equivalent money payments by the peasants as compensation for their freedom. Compensation payments by the peasants also contributed largely to the fortunes of landowners within the Hapsburg Empire. Not for the Prussian, Austrian, Bohemian, or Hungarian nobility any such emblem of weakness as the crop-lien credit system of the American South. Receptive to the needs of landowners, banks provided mortgage credit with which they could replace equipment formerly supplied by the serfs themselves, could engage in technological improvements, and—most important of all—could meet the cash payroll required by a change-over to wage labor. Because of the availability of bank credit, transitional forms such as labor service—roughly equivalent to share tenancy in the American South—lingered only briefly within the nations of the Austro-Hungarian monarchy. Large landowners soon had the resources to convert their work forces into a regulation wage-earning proletariat.[28]

The southern planters, who had largely controlled the antebellum southern banking system, could not exert comparable power after the debacle of the Confederacy. Indeed, their absence from the national government when the National Banking Acts were adopted during the war ensured that, whoever controlled it, the postwar southern banking system would be unequal to the exigent credit needs of postwar southern agriculture.[29] The uncompensated loss of slave property, bringing with it a dramatic plunge in the value of land, left southern landowners with scant collateral to offer lenders. Accordingly, credit arrangements consisted of a ramshackle structure in which credit advanced against a growing crop (the crop-lien system) supplemented credit in effect advanced by tenants who supplied their own implements, seed, and work stock, or by laborers who did not collect their wages until the end of a yearly contract period. Early in this century, mortage loans on landed property amounted to 33 to 40 percent of the value of arable land in Hungary, still more in Austria. An 1890 Senate report affords some notion of the difference in the American South, though the form of measurement is not strictly comparable: in Georgia, 3.38 percent of farms cultivated by their owners were mortgaged, and in South Carolina, 8 percent.[30] When southern agriculture did benefit substantially from the sort of mortgage credit that routinely supported agricultural capitalism in western or central Europe or the northern United States, the beneficiaries were not the old planter class, but a new and indubitably capitalist one.[31]

The "slow outward trickle of food and supplies and equipment" from the plantation commissary that "returned each fall as cotton made and ginned and sold" represented, in Faulkner's words, "two threads frail as truth and impalpable as equators yet cable-strong to bind for life them who made the cotton to the land their sweat fell on."[32] But that was the last, lowest link of a bondage equally strong to bind them that owned—or pretended to own—the land without having the ultimate power to decide its fate. The backward credit system of the postwar South held the planters in thrall as surely as the planters held those beneath them. In this respect the planters more closely resembled a decadent colonial ruling class, trading its national sovereignty for the right to exploit the local peasants, than they resembled proud Junkers or boyars, whose revolutionary defeat lay still in the future.

What is the "classic" route to capitalism anyway? If, as some historians seem to imply, the term refers only to the English and northern American pattern, then it quickly outdates itself and becomes a useless tool for understanding the past. The English agricultural revolution could happen only once, and the northern American version—occurring in a huge, sparsely populated[33] continent—could repeat itself only in the rare instance (for example, Australia) in which this situation was replicated. The demand of industrial or industrializing capitalist economies for agricultural commodities provided the economic impulse for the capitalist development of agriculture in eastern and central Europe, as in the postbellum American South. Under the depressed conditions prevailing during the late nineteenth century, the Prussian way (depending on the initiative of large landholders commanding the labor of landless or nearly landless peasants) proved a quicker and surer route to agricultural capitalism than the American (relying upon the evolution of free peasant agriculture). Capitalism emerged more quickly in the Austro-Hungarian monarchy than in the southern Balkans, dominated by smallholding peasant agriculture. Even differentiation within the peasantry itself, as a portion of the peasants became capitalists, happened faster where capitalism came under the aegis of large landowners.[34]

In the southern Balkans, which had been under Ottoman rule, the abolition of feudalism coincided with the departure of the Turkish landowners, who had exacted a tribute from the peasants without seriously disturbing the underlying structure of peasant agriculture. With the feudal upper class peeled away like a crust, peasant agriculture reemerged. Smallholdings dominated the countryside of Serbia and Bulgaria (and, for that matter, Greece). Rural communes, which traditionally redistributed land and enforced communal patterns of work, persisted through the nineteenth century in the southern Slavic areas. These raised a stubborn obstacle to the coming of capitalist agriculture by either the Prussian or the American route. As two Hungarian students of the question have remarked, "Communal peasant labor performed without payment or compensation prevented wage work from gaining ground, rendering it unnecessary and even impossible." The fate of the Balkan peasantry was, in general, abject poverty. Population growth eroded the size of holdings, while the weight of usurious credit and state taxation reduced many to a state of chronic indebtedness. The situation became worse as the traditional communal institutions slowly disintegrated, leaving the peasants without either the old forms of protection against utter destitution or the prospect of absorption by a growing capitalist economy.[35]

An interesting question arises about what might have happened if capitalism had arrived in the South by the so-called American route. That would have required the creation, in essence, of a black yeomanry: the confiscation of landed estates, the political suppression of their owners, and the distribution of land (as well as credit) to the freedmen and landless whites. Tremendous obstacles stood in the way of such a development. Leaving these aside, however, let us consider the probable results. Those among the liberators (probably a minority) who hoped to establish the freedmen as a black yeomanry most likely expected this yeomanry to follow the American path to agrarian capitalism rather than to withdraw itself, as the antebellum white yeomanry had done, into largely self-sufficient communities. What we know about the freedmen, however, suggests that most would have followed the latter course.

Mixed-farming peasant agriculture, geared to local or protected markets, showed remarkable resiliency during the depression that flattened those caught up in the world market for staple food crops and agricultural raw materials. An instructive point of reference is France, whose revolution erected such protections for petty-commodity peasant production and built the peasantry so inescapably into the structure of subsequent French regimes as to create a massive barrier to the advance of capitalist agriculture up to relatively recent times. Behind that protective screen, French peasants weathered the late-nineteenth-century depression rather successfully. Even today, the dying echo of their long resistance to incorporation into the roulette game of the capitalist world market may be heard whenever the ministers of the European Economic Community meet to discuss agricultural matters.[36]

Under similar conditions, a black yeomanry not only might have managed to stay afloat itself for a crucial interval; it might also, by blocking the reconstitution of the staple—especially cotton—economy, have afforded the white yeomanry enough breathing room to save its political and moral economy, as well as its economic economy, from the destruction all three suffered in the postbellum period. The respite could not have lasted forever. But suppose it had lasted for a while: how would the South have been different? For one thing, race relations would have been different, and probably better.[37] Of more direct relevance to the subject at hand, the advance of capitalist agriculture would have been greatly slowed, though not altogether stopped.

Notes

1.   The quotation comes from William Faulkner, *The Hamlet* (New York: Random House, 1956), 79. Faulkner's almost diabolical insight may, in this instance as in others, have led him to a trail along which historians and economists would do well to follow. For in our preoccupation with the automobile as the embodiment and pioneer of the mass-

market consumer durable, we have slighted the automobile's predecessor in this role, the sewing machine. I am indebted to Ernest Mandel for this suggestion.

2.   Rodney Hilton, *The Transition from Feudalism to Capitalism* (London: NLB, 1976), 14–17, 22–29, 161–63; C. H. George, "The Making of the English Bourgeoisie, 1500–1750," *Science and Society* 35 (Winter, 1971): 385–414; E. J. Hobsbawm, *The Age of Revolution, 1789–1848* (New York: New American Library, 1964), 22–43; Jerome Blum, *Our Forgotten Past: Seven Centuries of Life on the Land* (London: Thames and Hudson, 1982), 59.

3.   Hobsbawm, *Age of Revolution,* 29–31. The so-called "second serfdom" was not, however, a simple reflex of the world market, nor were the societies of eastern Europe the dependent periphery of a capitalist "world-system"—the market determinist position rehabilitated by Immanuel M. Wallerstein (*The Modern World-System: Capitalist Agriculture and the Origins of the European World-Economy in the Sixteenth Century* [New York, Academic, 1974]) and his considerable body of disciples. The possibility of trade with the West intensified feudal exploitation in parts of eastern Europe and provided it a continuing raison d'être, but did not originally bring it about. Not until capitalism reached its industrial phase, as Perry Anderson has correctly insisted, could it create a world market having the power to dominate the internal development of societies falling within its orbit (*Passages from Antiquity to Feudalism* [London: NLB, 1974], 229–64, and *Lineages of the Absolutist State* [London: NLB, 1974], 195–97). And even then, it is proper to add, the market alone cannot account for that internal development in all its details.

4.   The phrase "dual revolution" comes from Hobsbawm, whose *Age of Revolution* is a lucid and wide-ranging survey of the dual revolution's global consequences.

5.   Serfdom, or its equivalent, continued in parts of Latin America into the twentieth century, however. Persisting civil and political subordination of peasants in some parts of southern and eastern Europe, moreover, requires the qualification "formal" upon the liquidation of European serfdom. Ernesto Laclau, "Feudalism and Capitalism in Latin America" in *Politics and Ideology in Marxist Theory* (London: NLB, 1979), 15–50; Introduction to Kenneth Duncan and Ian Rutledge, eds., *Land and Labour in Latin America* (Cambridge: Cambridge Univ. Press, 1977), 1–20; E. J. Hobsbawm, *The Age of Capital, 1848–1875* (London: Weidenfeld and Nicolson, 1975), 183.

6.   Some economists prefer to define the Great Depression of the late nineteenth century out of existence, on the grounds that total world output suffered no outright decline. However, comparison with the periods before and after in two key particulars— the growth rate of industrial output and of world trade—shows that the preference is ill-advised. In any case, contemporaries who used the term *great depression* (especially the millions out of work during the worst years) had no comparable doubts. On worldwide implications of the depression, see Hans Rosenberg, "Political and Social Consequences of the Great Depression of 1873–1896 in Central Europe," *Economic History Review* 13 (1943): 58–73; E. J. Hobsbawm, *Labouring Men: Studies in the History of Labour* (New York: Basic Books, 1964), ch. 17; and Hobsbawm, *Age of Capital,* p. 5. On the rhythm of the world capitalist economy—the problem of the so-called long waves—see Ernest Mandel, *Long Waves in Capitalist Development: The Marxist Interpretation* (Cambridge: Cambridge University Press, 1980), based on the 1978 Alfred Marshall Lectures at Cambridge University; and Mandel, *Late Capitalism* (London: NLB, 1975), ch. 4.

7.   Annie Davis to Abraham Lincoln, Aug. 25, 1864, D-304 1864, Letters Received, ser. 360, Colored Troops Division, Records of the Adjutant General's Office, Record Group (RG) 94, National Archives (NA) [B-87]. The numbers in brackets, here and

hereafter, indicate the file number of the document copy housed at the Freedmen and Southern Society Project, University of Maryland, College Park, Maryland.

8.   Brig. Gen. J. W. Phelps to Capt. R. S. Davis, June 16, 1862, copied in J. W. Phelps report of service, Jan. 16, 1873, Generals' Reports of Service, vol. 6, Records of the Adjutant General's Office, 1780s–1917, ser. 160, RG 94, NA [JJ-5].

9.   Economists sometimes claim that this property was not abolished, but merely transferred to the freedmen. The formula generally invoked is that the ex-slaves acquired title to their "human capital." All such notions are mistaken. The abolition of slavery made liberty—in the language of the Declaration of Independence—"unalienable," and thus deprived it of a market value that could be transferred. The adoption of the Thirteenth Amendment meant that a human being in America could not sell his person, which is the only way his liberty could be construed to possess a market value. Thenceforward, he could sell only the product of his labor or his capacity for labor during a stipulated period. Such authors as Charles and Mary Beard, W. E. B. Du Bois, and James S. Allen have, whatever the necessary modifications to their conclusions, forced historians to come to terms with the revolutionary implications of the Civil War and Reconstruction, though their work continues to be the target of ill-tempered criticism. For example, Dan T. Carter has dismissed Allen's work as fit only for "readers with pronounced masochistic tendencies." The gratuitous discourtesy is the more noticeable because, in the same article, Carter takes Barrington Moore, Jr., to task for setting a "petulant standard" by "gracelessly" dismissing the work of a scholarly opponent. Dan T. Carter, "From the Old South to the New: Another Look at the Theme of Change and Continuity," in *From the Old South to the New: Essays on the Transitional South*, ed. Walter J. Fraser, Jr., and Winfred B. Moore, Jr. (Westport, Conn.: Greenwood, 1981), 26, 30, 31.

10.   A recent study (James Oakes, *The Ruling Race: A History of American Slaveholders* [New York: Knopf, 1982]) argues that small slaveholders, not planters, dominated southern society. This thesis is a virtual duplicate of the one Frank Owsley and his students advanced with respect to the non-slaveholders and is based on the same conceptual error: that numbers alone confer dominance. Were this so, the meek would long since have inherited the earth. The strictures of Fabian Linden ("Economic Democracy in the Slave South: An Appraisal of Some Recent Views," *Journal of Negro History* 31 [April, 1946]: 140–89) upon Owsley's school apply, with minor changes, to Oakes's argument.

11.   Jonathan M. Wiener, "Planter Persistence and Social Change: Alabama, 1850–1870," *Journal of Interdisciplinary History* 7 (Autumn, 1976): 235–60, and *Social Origins of the New South: Alabama, 1860–1885* (Baton Rouge, La., 1978); and Kenneth S. Greenberg, "The Civil War and the Redistribution of Land: Adams County, Mississippi, 1860–1870," *Agricultural History* 52 (April, 1978): 292–307, provide good examples of the empirical argument, which is probably sound as far as it goes. Greenberg shows exemplary caution in refusing to place upon the evidence a heavier interpretive weight than it can bear. Other distinguished proponents of the view that the planters' power derived from landownership include Jay R. Mandle (*The Roots of Black Poverty: The Southern Plantation Economy after the Civil War* [Durham, N.C.: Duke Univ. Press, 1978], and Alan Dawley, "E. P. Thompson and the Peculiarities of the Americans," *Radical History Review* 19 (Winter, 1978–79): 33–59. Dawley adds the twist of asserting that the planters' power rested first on land and later on slaves.

12.   W. E. B. Du Bois, "Of the Black Belt" and "Of the Quest of the Golden Fleece," in *The Souls of Black Folk* (New York: New American Library, 1969).

13.   C. Vann Woodward, *Origins of the New South, 1877–1913* (Baton Rouge: Louisiana State Univ. Press, 1971), 119–20, 179; Robert L. Brandfon, *Cotton Kingdom of the New South: A History of the Yazoo-Mississippi Delta from Reconstruction to the Twentieth Century* (Cambridge, Mass.: Harvard Univ. Press, 1967); Joseph P. Reidy, "The Development of Central Factories and the Rise of Tenancy in Louisiana's Sugar Economy, 1880–1910," paper delivered at annual meeting, Social Science History Association, Nov., 1982, Bloomington, Ind. Leslie S. Rowland kindly shared with me her unpublished work on the lowcountry rice industry. The writings of Alfred Holt Stone (see esp. "The Negro in the Yazoo-Mississippi Delta," *Publications of the American Economic Association*, 3rd ser., vol. 3 [New York, 1902], 235–78; "A Plantation Experiment," *Quarterly Journal of Economics* 19 [Feb., 1905]: 270–87) perfectly exemplify the standpoint of a new class of planters valiantly striving to establish an unbroken lineage with the paternalist regime of the Old South.

14.   Gavin Wright, *The Political Economy of the Cotton South: Households, Markets, and Wealth in the Nineteenth Century* (New York: Norton, 1978), 44–55. Witold Kula, *An Economic Theory of the Feudal System*, trans. Lawrence Garner (London: NLB, 1976), 72, 72–73n, makes the same point with respect to the feudal economy.

15.   Eugene D. Genovese, "Yeomen Farmers in a Slaveholders' Democracy," *Agricultural History* 44 (April, 1975): 331–42; *The Political Economy of Slavery: Studies in the Economy and Society of the Slave South* (New York: Random House, 1967), esp. ch. 7.

16.   Steven Hahn, "The Yeomanry in the Non-Plantation South: Upper Piedmont Georgia, 1850–1860," in Orville Vernon Burton and Robert C. McMath Jr., eds., *Class, Conflict, and Consensus: Antebellum Southern Community Studies* (Westport, Conn.: Greenwood, 1981). It has been suggested that the extraordinarily high price of slave property on the eve of the Civil War might constitute an "index of sanguinity," expressing southerners' confidence in the future; see Wright, *Political Economy*, 144–50. This argument is 180 degrees off. Someone might as well assert that the high price of a house today is an index of sanguinity for our own society.

17.   Michael P. Johnson, *Toward a Patriarchal Republic: The Secession of Georgia* (Baton Rouge: Louisiana State Univ. Press, 1977).

18.   Armstead Robinson's calculations (*Bitter Fruits of Bondage: Slavery's Demise and the Collapse of the Confederacy* [New Haven, Conn.: Yale Univ. Press, forthcoming]) demonstrate the fragility of the yeomen's economy, its vulnerability to natural or man-made calamity. The moral and ideological components of the yeomen's way of life were, of course, correspondingly vulnerable.

19.   Steven Hahn, *The Roots of Southern Populism: Yeoman Farmers and the Transformation of the Georgia Upcountry, 1850–1890* (New York: Oxford Univ. Press, 1983), ch. 5; "Hunting, Fishing, and Foraging and the Transformation of Property Rights in the Postbellum South," *Radical History Review* 26 (1982): 37–64; "Common Right and Commonwealth: The Stock-Law Struggle and the Roots of Southern Populism," in *Region, Race, and Reconstruction, Essays in Honor of C. Vann Woodward*, ed. J. Morgan Kousser and James M. McPherson (New York: Oxford Univ. Press, 1982). Gavin Wright and Howard Kunreuther's metaphor (it is no more than that) of farming as a game of chance ("Cotton, Corn and Risk in the Nineteenth Century," *Journal of Economic History* 35 [Sept., 1975]: 526–51) provides a serviceable device for understanding the purely economic results once the "game" has been set up. But it offers no consistent explanation of how sensible people come to be players in such a game, still less of their motives while seated at the table. The limitations of this approach receive consideration in Harold D. Woodman, "Sequel to Slavery: The New History Views the Postbellum

South," *Journal of Southern History* 43 (Nov., 1977): 523–54, and in my essay "The Nineteenth-Century American South: History and Theory," *Plantation Society in the Americas* 2 (April, 1983), 7–27.

20.   Harold D. Woodman, *King Cotton and his Retainers: Financing and Marketing the Cotton Crop of the South, 1800–1925* (Lexington: Univ. of Kentucky Press, 1968), ch. 23.

21.   Reidy, "Development of Central Factories"; Thavolia Glymph, "Wages, Share Wages, Sharecropping: The Transition from Slavery to Freedom in the Rural South, 1860–1880," (paper delivered at annual meeting, Association for the Study of Afro-American Life and History, Oct., 1976, Chicago); Woodman, "Sequel to Slavery," 551–52, and "Post–Civil War Southern Agriculture and the Law," *Agricultural History* 53 (Jan., 1979): 319–37. Conclusions concerning the lowcountry rice industry are based on Rowland's unpublished work (see n. 13 above).

22.   Joseph P. Reidy, review of Wiener's *Social Origins of the New South*, in *Science and Society* 46 (Spring, 1982): 97–100.

23.   Wiener propounds this argument with skill and persistence in "Class Structure and Economic Development in the American South, 1865–1955," *American Historical Review* 84 (Oct., 1979): 970–1006, as well as in *Social Origins of the New South: Alabama, 1860–1885* (Baton Rouge: Louisiana State Univ. Press, 1978).

24.   David Brion Davis, *The Problem of Slavery in Western Culture* (Ithaca, N.Y.: Cornell Univ. Press, 1966), 40; E. J. Hobsbawm, *Industry and Empire* (Baltimore: Penguin, 1969), 229, and *Age of Revolution*, 44–73, 185, 236–37.

25.   V. I. Lenin, "The Agrarian Question in Russia towards the Close of the Nineteenth Century," in *Collected Works*, vol. 15 (Moscow: Foreign Language Publishing House, 1963), 139–40.

26.   On the question of the public domain, see Henry Nash Smith, *Virgin Land: The American West as Symbol and Myth* (Cambridge, Mass.: Harvard Univ. Press, 1970), bk. 3; Paul W. Gates, *The Farmer's Age: Agriculture, 1800–1860* (1960; repr. White Plains, N.Y.: M. E. Sharpe, 1977), chap. 4. On the character of northern farming communities, see Christopher Clark, "Household Economy, Market Exchange, and the Rise of Capitalism in the Connecticut Valley, 1800–1860," *Journal of Social History* 13 (Winter, 1979): 169–89; James A. Henretta, "Families and Farms: *Mentalité* in Pre-Industrial America," *William and Mary Quarterly*, 3d ser. 35 (Jan., 1978): 3–32; Michael Merrill, "Cash is Good to Eat: Self-Sufficiency and Exchange in the Rural Economy of the United States," *Radical History Review* 3 (Winter, 1977): 42–71.

27.   Barrington Moore, Jr., *Social Origins of Dictatorship and Democracy: Lord and Peasant in the Making of the Modern World* (Boston: Beacon, 1966).

28.   Iván T. Berend and György Ránki, *East Central Europe in the 19th and 20th Centuries* (Budapest: Academiai Kiado, 1977), 11–40, and *Economic Development in East-Central Europe in the 19th and 20th Centuries* (New York: Columbia Univ. Press, 1974), chap. 2; Hobsbawm, *Age of Revolution*, 188, and *Age of Capital*, 188.

29.   Genovese, *Political Economy*, 21–22; Woodward, *Origins of the New South*, 183; Woodman, *King Cotton*, 345–47; John A. James, Financial Underdevelopment in the Postbellum South," *Journal of Interdisciplinary History* 11 (Winter, 1981): 443–54.

30.   Berend and Ránki, *Economic Development*, ch. 2; Fred A. Shannon, *The Farmer's Last Frontier: Agriculture, 1860–1897* (1945; repr. White Plains, N.Y.: M. E. Sharpe, 1977), 95.

31.   An example is the Delta and Pine Land Company, an English-owned cotton-growing enterprise capitalized at some three million dollars when it was formed and op-

erating in the Yazoo-Mississippi delta. See Brandfon, *Cotton Kingdom*, 128–31; Wood-man, "Postbellum Social Change and its Effects on Marketing the South's Cotton Crop," *Agricultural History* 56 (Jan., 1982): 219–22.

32.   William Faulkner, "The Bear," in *Go Down, Moses* (New York: Random House, 1973), 256.

33.   That sparseness was enhanced, it is hardly necessary to add, by the decimation of the aboriginal inhabitants.

34.   Berend and Rânki, *Economic Development*, 50, and *East Central Europe*, 33; Hobsbawm, *Age of Capital*, 188.

35.   Hobsbawm, *Age of Revolution*, 30; Berend and Rânki, *Economic Develop-ment*, 37–39, 49–50, and *East Central Europe*, 35–36.

36.   Hobsbawm, *Age of Revolution*, 93, 213, and *Age of Capital*, 178, 182.

37.   I have considered the consequences for racial ideology that such a develop-ment might have borne in "Ideology and Race in American History" in Kousser and McPherson, *Region, Race, and Reconstruction*, 166–68. Besides erecting an obstacle to southern capitalist development, the consolidation of a black yeomanry would have, at the least, required some readjustments in northern industry. A secure base in the countryside would have closed off the northern migration of black labor at its source. There is no empirical justification for the assumption, shared by writers as diverse in their ideological inspiration as Robert Higgs and Jay Mandle, that black southerners were perpetually poised on the edge of migration, either waiting until it was clearly prof-itable to move or prevented by illiteracy, the racism of northern employers, and the co-ercive control of southern planters (Robert Higgs, *Competition and Coercion: Blacks in the American Economy, 1865–1914* [Cambridge: Cambridge Univ. Press, 1977], 24–32; Mandle, *Roots of Black Poverty*, 16). Freedmen and their descendants went to extraordi-nary lengths to gain an independent base on the land and persisted in the teeth of re-peated defeats, as Ned Cobb (Nate Shaw) makes magnificently clear (*All God's Dangers: The Life of Nate Shaw*, ed. Theodore Rosengarten [New York: Knopf, 1974]). For them, as it had been for the English surplus rural population and as it would be for the eastern European surplus rural population, mass migration or emigration was the last resort when the rural economy could no longer accommodate them.

HAROLD D. WOODMAN

The Reconstruction of the Cotton Plantation in the New South

MY title is deliberately designed to evoke a familiar event, Reconstruction, and a familiar institution, the cotton plantation—but by juxtaposing them, to suggest an unfamiliar connection between the two.

From the beginning, Reconstruction was hotly debated. If the victorious northerners could agree that the Union had to be reconstructed after four years of war, they could not agree on how that task was to be accomplished. The central question seemed simple enough: how much change in the South was required to insure that military victory would be sustained in peacetime? When, in the midst of war, northern politicians began to discuss it, however, they found no simple answer. Once the war was over, southerners entered the debate, making an answer even more elusive. Solutions to the problem came only after long and bitter political struggle in which, among other things, President Andrew Johnson was impeached and very nearly convicted. The southern states, under military supervision, wrote new constitutions that ended slavery, repudiated the Confederate debt, and granted the vote to black men. Congress deemed governments elected under the new constitutions to be reconstructed and permitted them to send representatives to Washington. But the new state governments, Republican and interracial, had short lives. Torn by internal divisions and subjected to violence, intimidation, racism, and stuffed ballot boxes, they lost elections to a coalition of Democrats and conservatives who promised to "redeem" the South, ending corruption and the threat of black domination by returning control to the region's traditional white rulers. The last of the Republican governments disappeared in 1877 as part of the compromise that put Republican Rutherford B. Hayes in the White House and brought federal troops home from the South. Reconstruction was officially over.[1]

But the debate was not. For more than half a century the redeemers' version of events dominated historical writings. Historians depicted the years of radical rule as a time of unrelieved corruption when ignorant blacks, dishonest northerners, and a few turncoat southern whites brought the South to the brink of ruin. Although W. E. B. Du Bois as early as 1910 wrote of the "benefits" of Reconstruction,[2] it was not until later that the redeemer version of Reconstruction history came under systematic revision. The early-twentieth-century race relations movement, the civil rights struggles of blacks and their white allies, and the flood of civil rights legislation and court rulings (promptly dubbed "the second reconstruction") helped to stimulate new research into virtually every aspect of Reconstruction history. The new work, called "revisionist" because it revised the traditional interpretation, questioned every detail of the redeemer version of Reconstruction. At first the revisionists merely turned the older version on its head: villains became heroes and heroes, villains. But soon revisionists themselves were being revised as historians asked new questions, adopted new perspectives, and used new methods.[3]

Despite all their new work, revisionists shared with traditionalists a political approach to Reconstruction. Although they did not ignore such social and economic issues as the land question, civil rights for blacks, education, and taxation, they nevertheless subordinated these issues to partisan politics. The very definition of "the Reconstruction period" as the years between federal occupation and Redeemer victory dictated a political emphasis for the simple reason that these were political events.[4]

But southerners had to deal with another reconstruction, not unrelated to politics, but both more immediate and longer lasting: they had to reconstruct their economy and society. The easiest task was to repair the buildings, railroads, lands, and equipment damaged by war and neglect. But constructing a new economic system based on free labor proved far more difficult. In antebellum times, slavery had mobilized the region's labor force. Emancipation required a new system of labor mobilization. Whereas planters had previously commanded labor power by owning the laborers, they now had to get the labor power they needed by enticing it—that is, by buying it from laborers who remained free to choose to whom to sell their time and work.

If most historians have failed to appreciate how profoundly revolutionary was the change from slave to free labor, and how difficult it was to achieve, it may be that they, like the rest of us and, as we shall see, like contemporary northerners, have taken the free labor system for granted, as if it were somehow natural and unlearned. For example, we can easily forget how much of our education and training is really ideological, immersing us in ideas of responsibility, independence, self-reliance, and the opportunity to succeed along with notions of what will be expected of us when we reach adulthood. To be sure, in recent years a group calling themselves "new" labor and social historians have tried to trace the creation of a modern working class from a rural, pre-industrial, and often precapitalist population.[5] But these scholars have largely ignored the postbellum South. Although their concern has been with the creation of an industrial rather than a rural working class, it is nevertheless surprising that neither they nor others have attempted to apply their insights to the postbellum South, where former slaves and self-sufficient yeomen became members of a free working class on the region's farms and in its mills and factories.

This neglect arises partly from the continuing emphasis on the political aspect of Reconstruction. Such an emphasis, as I have already suggested, obscures the pattern of economic reconstruction; the 1877 terminal date makes it impossible to follow important economic and social changes that extend considerably beyond that date. Moreover, historians who have studied the post-1877 period in the South have continued to stress political rather than social and economic developments. As late as 1971, Charles Dew, after a long and detailed survey of the literature, concluded that "the economic history of the New South remains an undeveloped area of scholarship."[6]

But it is not merely the neglect of social and economic history that explains the failure to see and appreciate the revolutionary changes brought by the Civil War and emancipation. In the last decade the economic history of the nineteenth-century South has finally received considerable attention, but most of this work denies fundamental change and instead tends to emphasize continuity between old and new, finding little real change in the South before the New Deal and the massive exodus during and following World War II. The authors of these studies differ sharply in emphasis, method, and interpretation; yet in their sometimes angry debates,[7] they fail to notice how much, in the end, they all accept the theme of continuity.

I do not mean to minimize the differences that divide these scholars, for they paint vastly different pictures of the postwar South. For one group, the economy was backward and repressive, the former slaves and an increasing number of former yeomen held in thralldom by planters and merchants who exercised unrestrained economic and political power. The South was poor because the small group in control forced the overproduction of cotton and blocked economic diversification, thereby increasing their wealth at the expense of the majority of the population. Racism and the specter of black domination kept the poor and exploited majority of blacks and whites from uniting to improve their condition.[8] Another group describes a situation almost completely the reverse. Its members agree that the South was poor, and they do not deny the existence of violence and intimidation. But they do deny that the southern economy was stagnant and that planters and merchants had the ability—or, for that matter, the need—to interfere with the free market that determined optimal distribution of resources and labor. The region's poverty resulted from the economic losses incident to war and its immediate aftermath. Once back in operation, the free market produced optimal results in terms of income, wealth, and general well-being, but a half-century was not enough time to overcome wartime losses; therefore, the South, although it was catching up to the rest of the nation, remained poor.[9]

It would be difficult to imagine two evaluations of the same events and circumstances more different than those I have briefly described. Yet as I have already noted, these two approaches share the concept of continuity. They disagree as to what continued, however. Those in the first group find the repressive labor system of slavery continuing into the postwar period and engulfing not only blacks but many whites as well. Those in the second group find the free market, which had led to a wise allocation of resources under the slave regime, continuing into the postwar period with similarly beneficial resource allocation, the only hitch being the momentary, though massive, interference with that free market caused by the Civil War.

It is important to note that the economic historians' emphasis on continuity is paralleled by that of many who study Reconstruction in purely political terms. If the traditionalists viewed the radical rule as potentially revolutionary, so too do the revisionists. Where the traditionalists greeted redemption as the return to honest government and an end of revolutionary dangers, the revisionists see redemption as a return of rule to the prewar power elite and the failure to institute needed reforms. Both, then, could see Reconstruction as a tragedy, the first for what it might have done but luckily did not, the second for what it might have done but unfortunately did not. In either case, they see the period of radical control as brief; once ended, continuity prevailed.

As this brief historiographic survey makes clear, substantial evidence supports the view that continuity is the major theme in nineteenth-century southern history. It would appear, therefore, that my earlier use of the term "revolutionary" to describe the effects of the Civil War and emancipation is completely inappropriate. At best it might be used to describe the possibility for change favored by some who ultimately did not prevail. Freedmen received neither land nor mules, and they failed to keep their political rights. Freedom became a mockery when the lyncher's rope replaced the slaveowner's lash, debt servitude replaced slavery, and racism justified repression just as it had justified slavery. King Cotton remained on his throne, and the South, except in a few scattered places, did not experience the rapid industrial and commercial expansion that took place elsewhere in the nation.

That there is considerable evidence for continuity in the nineteenth-century South should not be surprising. The Civil War neither destroyed nor dispersed the people, black and white. Obviously, the world these people built after the war was heavily influenced by the legacy of the antebellum world, the only one they knew. Indeed, it is my argument that the only way to understand social and economic reconstruction is to appreciate the importance of this legacy as it affected the course of a fundamental and revolutionary transformation of the South. The task is not to compare a list showing changes with another showing continuity in order to determine which one best characterizes the nineteenth-century South. Comparing such lists inevitably leads to the convenient and liberal-minded conclusion that there was both continuity and change, a resolution that merely leaves the question unanswered.[10]

Instead of chronicling quantity, we must rather assess quality: the problem is not how *much* change but what *kind* of change. Those who count persisting planters and Whigs, or list persisting evidences of racism or persisting patterns of coercion, are not so much wrong as incomplete in their analyses, because they ignore the social revolution initiated by and required by emancipation: a slave society had to be transformed into a bourgeois, free labor society.[11] The Civil War and emancipation achieved only half a revolution; they destroyed an old economic system but created nothing to replace it. Moreover, this destructive half of the revolution, although it had supporters within the South (most notably the blacks but also some whites), did not result from an internal upheaval by a class armed with the experience, the ideology, and the vision of a new society. It was imposed from the outside. Thus, the remaining half of the revolution, the building of a free labor economy and society, had to be achieved by a population that had not initiated the revolution in the first place—indeed, by a population that included large numbers who actively and violently opposed it. This alone would explain evidences of continuity.

But these elements of continuity do not signal counterrevolution. Slavery was gone. Slaves who had been chattel became free workers; planters who had been slaveowners producing a single crop for a world market, and a food supply that made their plantations self-sufficient rural centers of power, became businessmen, employers of free labor, and investors in agricultural, industrial, and commercial enterprises; whites who had never owned slaves, who had produced a rude if ample self-sufficiency on their small farms, became commercial farmers, mill hands, and industrial workers. Such massive social changes can only be described as revolutionary.

To say that slaves became free workers is not to deny that they were subjected to violence, intimidation, and other forms of coercion; or that their freedom of choice was often the choice between one kind of work and starvation; or that their living and working conditions were wretched. But such language could also be, and was, applied to the condition of the working class in the North, in England, in France, and elsewhere at the time. A casual glance at the reformist literature of the late nineteenth century makes it clear that the South had no monopoly on coercing and underpaying workers, or on company stores and company towns.[12] Even if it could be shown that the treatment of blacks was worse than that of northern workers, it would not follow that blacks were not free workers. That they were "free" means that they were no longer property to be bought, sold, traded, and moved at the whim of their owners, and that they were no longer wealth to serve as collateral for loans or as symbols of prestige and power. Only if we equate free labor with freedom in its democratic and equalitarian sense will we have difficulty seeing and appreciating the importance of the change from slavery to free labor.

That the change, when stated in this way, seems obvious does not make it unimportant. That former slaveowners had difficulty accepting the change, or that freedmen understood it quite differently from their former owners and their northern liberators, does not mean it did not take place. Emancipation created the necessary condition for the rise of a free labor system, but it was not sufficient in itself to create that system immediately. Such a system requires that there be a market for labor power rather than for laborers themselves, but this in turn requires a set of institutions and perceptions and an ideology that allow that market to function. The conflicts and struggles in the postwar South may be best understood as arising from tensions between an inherited ideology based on slavery and the need to forge the institutions necessary for a free labor system. If we start with the obvious yet fundamental change from slavery to free labor and then recognize that southerners, black and white, had to complete the revolution begun by emancipation by building a free labor society, we can begin to make sense of the confusing and often contradictory evidence we find in our investigations of the postwar years: the great variety of early tenure forms; the tentativeness and variability in early laws regarding liens and tenancy; the conflicts among merchants, planters, yeomen, and blacks over rights and duties; the nature and extent of violence and coercion. What appears to be confusion often approaching anarchy becomes comprehensible when we recognize that people held varying views shaped by a past experience that had become irrelevant. They were looking backward as they stumbled uncertainly into the future.

For many of the victorious northerners, the future did not seem uncertain—at least not at first. Those who went south to work with the freedmen were filled with enthusiasm and confidence. Once released from the shackles of slavery, the blacks, they thought, would respond like free people everywhere, would be eager to work because they would now reap the benefits of their toil. True, slavery had kept them in the grossest ignorance and had linked labor and servitude, but proper schools and adequate returns from their work would help them overcome slavery's pernicious legacy quickly and easily. Motivated by an evangelical humanitarianism, they came south, opened schools, and (in Horace Mann Bond's words) provided the blacks with "moral homilies . . . in the best New England Sunday School style," reflecting the "youthful industrialism of the North" in the prewar generation in which they had grown up.[13]

The benefit of hindsight informed Bond's cynicism about Sunday School homilies, but his recognition of the source of these ideas remains a significant insight. By the mid-nineteenth century, a free labor ideology had become pervasive in the North.[14] It was a view that stressed the dignity of labor and the opportunities available to those who worked hard and were honest and faithful. It described the system itself; as David Montgomery has noted, "the nation's economic system was not called 'capitalism' but the 'free-labor system.'"[15] And this system, northerners insisted, stood in marked contrast to that in the South. As Daniel T. Rodgers observes, northerners "saw themselves as a society of hard-working and economically independent farmers, mechanics, and tradesmen, defending the cause of a worker's freedom against the inroads of the Southern master-servant economy."[16]

The Union victory was a victory for the free labor system, and its benefits now had to be extended to the South, proclaimed the Indiana radical, George W. Julian:

> Instead of large estates, widely scattered settlements, wasteful agriculture, popular ignorance, political and social degradation, the decay of literature, the decline of manufactures and the arts, contempt for honest labor, and a pampered aristocracy, we must have small farms, closely associated communities, thrifty tillage, free schools, social independence, a healthy literature, flourishing manufactures and mechanic arts, respect for honest labor, and equality of political rights.[17]

These Sunday School homilies were heard in the halls of Congress and from the lecture platform, read in the press, and absorbed in the schoolroom. Every child who learned his letters from McGuffey's ubiquitous readers learned also the message of the free labor ideology:

> Work, work, my boy, be not afraid;
>   Look labor boldly in the face;
> Take up the hammer or the spade,
>   And blush not for your humble place. . . .

I doubt if he who lolls his head
Where idleness and plenty meet,
Enjoys his pillow or his bread
As those who earn the meals they eat.[18]

If such descriptions of the free labor ideology sound naive to the modern ear and, indeed, were already becoming anachronistic at the time,[19] they seemed natural and self-evident to those who expressed them. But when it came time to create a free labor system in the South, differences arose among advocates of free labor. Men such as Julian envisioned a South of small, independent farmers and merchants, while others, equally ardent supporters of a free labor system, emphasized the need to get southerners back to work producing the valuable staple crops, particularly cotton.

Businessman Edward Atkinson, for example, saw no contradiction between large-scale commercial production of cotton and the free labor system; indeed the two supported each other and would at the same time benefit all, while ending forever the menace of the servile labor system that had threatened national unity. "It is already evident," he wrote in 1864, "that the whole cotton country must be permeated and regenerated by New England men and by New England ideas, and that by their work the cultivation of cotton . . . will be developed to its fullest extent."[20] He reasoned that if cotton could be produced under slavery, "a system of labor so utterly false by all rules of sound political economy," then free labor, in harmony with "the highest morality and the strictest justice to the most humble of its people," would surely be more successful. The experiment at Port Royal proved that such theories were solidly grounded in reality. Early in the war federal troops occupied the Sea Islands off the coast of South Carolina, and there blacks, sometimes working on their own and sometimes under the direction of northerners, returned to work as free workers. Quoting at length from a March 3, 1864, article in the *New York Evening Post* by Edward S. Philbrick, one of the northerners directing work in the area, Atkinson concluded that Sea Island blacks, "probably the most difficult portion of their race to be dealt with, because of their entirely isolated and absolutely ignorant condition," had proved to be able and willing workers who produced a good quality of cotton for the New York market. What was done on the Sea Islands

could be done everywhere in the South. Therefore, Atkinson concluded, "the negro question is solved."[21]

With the South's major problem solved, Atkinson envisioned the
rise of a pastoral free labor utopia with a happy and prosperous population blessed by God and snugly clad in New England textiles:

> Then picture this land as it shall surely be in a few years hence, — the land
> divided, if not by confiscation, then by the operation of the ordinary work-
> ing of our system of land tenure (for with the restoration of the State comes
> back the mortgage for foreclosure, or the need that the owner shall sell a
> portion of his land in order that he may be able to use the remainder), —
> the freedmen developing, as at Port Royal, the desire to become land-
> owners, and enabled to become so by the large profits which the next few
> years must yield to all cultivators of cotton, — villages established, — the
> Yankee school-teacher everywhere at work, — the men in the fields, — the
> women in their own homes, — the children at school, — none clad now in
> coarse hand-made fabrics, but in New England manufactures purchased
> and paid for with their own money, — the poor white trash no longer re-
> pelled and forced to spread over southern Illinois and Indiana the darkness
> of Egypt, but at home slowly and surely learning that true independence
> which they now honestly but blindly seek under the false lead of the
> Slaveholder of the South and the Copperhead of the North, — and every-
> where the church spire pointing its finger toward heaven, leading up to the
> one Infinite Power which is now guiding this nation through sorrow and
> tribulation — the atonement for its great national crime — to liberty and
> union eternal as the heavens.[22]

Here was a complete statement of the free labor ideology that was
both visionary and intensely practical. Released from the incubus of
slavery, blacks and whites alike would prosper, and the danger of dis-
unity would be over forever. Moreover, Atkinson made clear, there was
no need for further interference with southern property. Emancipation made confiscation of land unnecessary because those who had too
much would readily sell their surplus land to those who had too little,
and both would benefit. Enlightened self-interest would induce hard
work, good incomes, and increasing wealth, while the free market
would ensure mutually advantageous exchange of goods and services.

Furthermore, this enlightened self-interest—that is, the search for
maximum profits—would mean the production of cotton to supply the
needs of the hungry mills of the North and Europe. There was no need
for blacks or poor whites to flee the South; they could, and should, remain and turn their region into a southern New England, complete

with the familiar churches. But it would be a rural, agricultural New England; it would have church spires and schools but not mills and factories. In the New England industrialist's vision of the future, the South would continue to grow cotton, and New England would continue to manufacture cloth.

It would be a mistake to dismiss Atkinson's depiction of independent, landowning farmers producing a valuable and profitable commercial crop as mere rhetoric to hide his primary concern: the production of cotton for New England's mills. True, the free labor system as envisioned by Atkinson did not develop in the South, but at the same time the economy in the North lost whatever similarity it had to the model upon which Atkinson based his vision. Both changed radically, but by the end of the century the southern economy bore a striking resemblance to that in the North. Economic reconstruction had transformed most former slaves and many former yeomen into a working class, and had turned many former slaveowners and some others into businessmen. "Reconstruction" in the title of this essay refers to this economic transformation; the "plantation" refers to the central institution in agriculture that resulted.

The basic assumption in the free labor ideology was that people would work without physical compulsion because it was in their own interest to do so. Slavery was socially debilitating because slaves worked merely to avoid punishment. Free people worked harder and more reliably than slaves because they reaped the benefits of their work. With each individual working for his own gain, the entire society would benefit from the resulting increase in total output and wealth. Thus, what Adam Smith had called the "invisible hand" would guide the South to the end that Atkinson had described.

The means to get the process underway seemed obvious, at least to northerners such as Atkinson. Southerners had the land, the labor, and the knowhow to produce cotton. Prices for the staple were high, indicating strong demand. Given such conditions, the rest would be automatic. This explains his initial enthusiasm, but it does not explain what actually happened.

If the general proposition were true that people will voluntarily work for their own benefit (even if that benefit be merely the avoidance of starvation), "it did not follow," as Thomas C. Holt has put it, "that freedmen would apply themselves to the production of plantation staples or that their labor would be disciplined and reliable."[23] Nor did it follow that their potential employers, the planters who had owned them as chattel, would know how to deal with the freedmen as employees.

Experience soon revealed problems. A scant year after Atkinson had enthusiastically declared that "the negro question is solved," prospects looked far less rosy. Edward Philbrick, whose report had helped fire Atkinson's enthusiasm, now viewed matters more soberly: "The change is too great a one to be made in a day. It will take many years to make an economical and thrifty man out of a freedman, and about as long to make a sensible and just employer out of a former slaveholder."[24]

From all over the South, Freedmen's Bureau officials reported much the same story. Although they retained their faith in the free labor system, their work in the field demonstrated that the system was not easily applied. "It is a subject of congratulation," reported John C. Robinson from North Carolina, "to see the great good that has been accomplished in the elevation of a race of people to a sphere which their habits and education, and the opposition of their former owners made it extremely difficult for them to understand." Similarly, R. K. Scott concluded his report from South Carolina by noting that the "free labor of the past year in this State, notwithstanding the ignorance of the freedmen, the want of capital, and the impracticable views of land owners, has demonstrated the fact that the same incentive which prompts the white man of the north and other countries to labor will apply to the freedmen of the south."[25]

It was apparent that the mere absence of slavery did not ensure the presence of a liberal bourgeois economy. The free market would operate only if people acted as they were supposed to. But, alas, southerners—black and white—did not. Slavery turned out to be more than a legal relationship; it had social and psychological dimensions that did not disappear with the passage of a law or a constitutional amendment. People had to learn how to respond—perhaps even be coerced.

Such was the conclusion of one Captain Charles Soule, head of a "Special Commission on Contracts with Freedmen at Orangeburg, S.C.," who in mid-1865 called together the local freedmen and read them a carefully prepared speech designed to explain the duties and responsibilities of free people and to disabuse them of a number of pernicious ideas that the blacks, in their naiveté, might confuse with freedom. He told the assembled freedmen that their duty was to work hard and obey orders. He warned them not to expect that freedom would automatically ensure the good life: "You are now free," he said, "but you must know that the only difference you can feel yet, between slavery and freedom, is that neither you nor your children can be bought or sold. You may have a harder time this year than you have ever had before; it will be the price you pay for freedom."

Blacks might have wondered about the value of freedom that had such a high price. Their wonder probably increased when Soule informed them that they not only had to work harder but had to do much the same work they had done as slaves. "Do not think, because you are free you can choose your own kind of work," he warned, explaining that "every man has his own place, his own trade that he was brought up to, and he must stick to it." For blacks, this place was work as fieldhands or house servants. There was no shame in such labor: "If a man works, no matter in what business, he is doing well. The only shame is to be idle and lazy."

Soule then went on to provide a cogent analysis of how the free labor system worked:

> You do not understand why some of the white people who used to own you, do not have to work in the field. It is because they are rich. If every man were poor, and worked in his own field, there would be no big farms, and very little cotton or corn raised to sell; there would be no money, and nothing to buy. Some people must be rich, to pay the others, and they have the right to do no work except to look out after their property. It is so everywhere.

The assembled blacks were probably surprised to learn that "it is so everywhere," for the free labor system that Soule described seemed no different from the slave system from which they had expected to be freed. But Soule noted what to him was a big difference: "Perhaps," he explained, "by hard work some of you may by-and-by become rich yourselves."

Soule sent a copy of his speech to Maj. Gen. O. O. Howard, the head of the Freedmen's Bureau. In a covering letter he explained to Howard that their experiences as slaves had failed to equip blacks with the proper attitudes. They refused fair contracts for work, took time off from their labors, were generally idle and often vicious—all vices that he attributed "not so much to their race, as to the system of slavery under which they had lived." The rigorous discipline of the plantation is gone, he explained, leaving blacks with nothing but the vices associated with slavery. Therefore, the new regime required a new "code of laws and punishments" to destroy slavery's vices and to teach the blacks by experience new patterns of behavior. "Only actual suffering, starvation, and punishment will drive many of them to work."

Soule found no reason to be apprehensive about the attitude of the former slaveowners. Deprived of their slaves, they had no choice but to turn to free labor to work their fields—and this, he said, was exactly what they were trying to do. He admitted that deep in the countryside some planters continued to treat the blacks as slaves, but such behavior would disappear as soon as the blacks became responsible workers, aware of their obligations.

Soule patterned his vision of the future of the South on his perception of the good society in the North—a disciplined, responsible, and energetic working class, adequately but not extravagantly paid, willingly and cheerfully accepting the direction of employers. He was not advocating a return to slavery; he would have been outraged if so charged. He was advocating a thoroughly bourgeois relation between capital and labor. The planters' offers of housing, food, clothing, and sometimes a small portion of the crop were certainly fair and adequate wages, he argued. After all, he explained, laborers in the North usually spent their entire wages for food, clothing, and house rent. If the freedmen received more, "the relation between capital and labor would be disturbed."[26] Critics in the North were already terming such conditions "wage slavery," but no such idea troubled Soule.

General Howard, both more sensitive and more perceptive than his subordinate, congratulated Soule for his efforts "to secure harmony and good will in society." He did not object to Soule's advice to the freedmen, but added mildly that "while we show the freedmen how freemen support themselves at the North by labor, we ought to let him [sic] taste somewhat of the freeman's privileges." The planters, he warned, wanted to deny the freedmen those privileges by imposing a "despotism" that was very close to slavery, and they expected the federal authorities to grant them the necessary authority and backing to do so. He gently chided his subordinate for being deceived by the planters' "sophistries," suggesting that they too required attention. If former slaves lacked the experience of free workers and needed Soule's earnest advice, former slaveowners were "mostly ignorant of the work-

ings of free labor," and needed advice as well: "You had better therefore draw up an address to them also explaining their duties and
obligations."[27]

The Civil War and emancipation had destroyed traditional lines of
authority, leaving the chaos and uncertainty that so troubled people
such as Soule. Emancipation without any form of payment or other
support for the freed slaves (beyond the temporary relief offered by
the army and the Freedmen's Bureau, relief that was niggardly to begin
with and withdrawn as quickly as possible for fear of weakening the
work ethic among blacks)[28] meant that the ex-slaves had no choice but
to go to work on the farms and plantations of their former owners.
Northerners saw this as the first step in the creation of a free labor society—even after they recognized that the change would not proceed
as smoothly as they had hoped and expected, and even when they disagreed about the sources of the problems that arose. New lines of authority had to be established, but by whom and to what end remained
uncertain.

The old planters found their accustomed authority challenged from
every direction—by blacks, by Freedmen's Bureau officials, by enterprising merchants, by radicals in the state legislatures, by Washington,
and—most debilitating of all—by their own inability to cope with
changed conditions.[29] Hiring laborers cost money, which the factors
upon whom they had always relied were often unable to supply, especially after initial crop failures made it impossible to repay loans. The
blacks frequently proved unreliable, leaving the fields at crucial times
to work for others who promised higher pay—an action that seemed
reasonable enough to those learning the oft repeated lessons about the
operation of the free labor market, but completely unreasonable to
those with a crop to care for and no workers in the fields.

In an attempt to improve the situation, planters offered to pay
workers a share of what they produced instead of a monthly cash wage.
They thought that workers would be more industrious if they shared in
the output and would not leave before the harvest for fear of forfeiting
their wages. Furthermore, under this arrangement planters could proceed with a minimum of operating expenses because most of the workers' wages would not be paid until the crop was picked and sold. As this
system became popular, it intensified the problems instead of solving
them and created new and unexpected difficulties. When crop failures

meant that there was nothing to be divided, employees became understandably reluctant to contract again on the same terms. Many workers complained that planters, despite the agreements, failed to pay them their share or drove them away after the crop was made but before the sale and division of proceeds. Planters, for their part, charged that workers would steal cotton from the fields and trade it for goods at local stores, where the merchants gave little thought to who owned the cotton they were buying in small parcels, often in the dead of night.

Other problems, new and confusing, arose. Workers insisted that their contracts called for the making of a particular crop, and they refused to do extra work—fencing, ditching, and other general maintenance as well as preparation of the fields for the next season—without extra pay. When planters sought to include these services in the contracts, the blacks simply declined to work for them. In brief, the blacks expected freedom to mean that they would no longer be treated like slaves. They opposed the planters' demands that they work the same hours, exert the same effort, and obey the same rules as they had as slaves. They demanded the right to work fewer hours, to allow their women to remain at home, to come and go as they pleased, and even to have a voice in the management of production—arguing that if they shared in the output, they should have a share in decisions that influenced that output. Some went so far as to claim that not only were they no longer slaves, but neither had they become employees or tenants; rather their new status made them partners in the enterprise.

Planters, to their disgust and chagrin, found themselves competing for the services of their former slaves by offering higher wages or a larger share of the crop, by promising to provide a school on the plantation, by providing food and clothing for both the men and their families, even when the women and children did not work in the fields. Workers resisted gang labor under close supervision as being no improvement over slavery. Unable to secure their own land, they sought increased independence in other ways, and learned to organize and withhold their labor until their demands were met. Some organized "companies," agreeing to work as a group on a particular parcel of land under their own supervision. Others sought to rent or lease land and work it themselves. Many refused to live in the old slave-quarter cabins, preferring to live in town, in their own communities, or scattered on the lands they worked.[30]

Edwin De Leon, an ardent and early advocate of the "New South," presented a gloomy picture of conditions in 1874. The causes of the general social disorganization, he perceptively noted, "have been partly political and partly produced by the effects of the earthquake shock which overturned the whole system of Southern life and labor, and the struggle to substitute a new one." Southern progress, he insisted, depended upon social stability. "The great, the vital question for the Southern cotton and sugar-growing region is the question of labor, and its regulation so as to make it profitable to employer and employed." Although he could not predict how this "vital question" would be solved, he did find hopeful signs, the most important being the fall of the radical state governments.[31]

Although they might not have been clear to De Leon, writing in 1874, changes were already underway. Hindsight allows us to see the growth and consolidation of a new dominant class made up of some elements of the old planter aristocracy and some newcomers who were able to capitalize on the new conditions. A number of historians have noted what they call the "persistence" of planters in the new South and have found this to be the basis for what they consider the persistence of old South values and perceptions in the new South.[32] But such a view ignores the fundamental change that was taking place. More important than the genealogy of the new class was the changed ideology of its members and their changed relationship to the means of production. Planters—at least those who survived and prospered—became businessmen, as did a growing merchant class that acquired large landholdings in the countryside. For many such capitalist landlords, land became but one in a portfolio of investments that included stores, gins, compresses, lumbering operations, and other businesses, as well as holdings in railroads, banks, and factories and speculation in the market, especially in cotton futures. Although this new class owed its wealth primarily to the agricultural sector (which remained overwhelmingly the most important in the southern economy), its orientation was urban, toward market and trade centers.[33] Some were absentee landlords, living in town and relying on others to supervise their lands and collect rents, while they devoted their energies to other economic pursuits. Others resided in the rural areas, turning dusty little crossroads villages into nerve centers for the direction of agricultural production, financing, marketing, and research.

Corresponding to these changes were similarly significant changes in the working class. The first step in solving what De Leon called "the great, the vital" problem of the South—the organization and discipline of the labor force—was in a very real sense a compromise: the recognition and acceptance of the fact that the blacks would not continue to work in gangs under strict supervision as they had as slaves. Wage labor on plantations of the prewar type gave way to what can be called share wages, whereby workers were paid a share of what they produced, but as I have already noted, this system did not have the results the planters expected. Gradually, in some instances, share wages evolved into tenancy; that is, payment *by* the landlord of a portion of the crop as wages became payment *to* the landlord of a portion of the crop as rent. Other, less unusual forms of tenancy also arose: payment of a set amount of cotton for use of the land (standing rent), and payment of an agreed amount of cash per acre for use of the land (money rent). At the same time, in other instances, share wages came to be called sharecropping. The sharecropper was not a tenant but a wage worker whose wages—a share of what he produced on a given parcel of land—were paid *to* him by the landowner.[34]

Changes came gradually, piecemeal, experimentally; they were compromises between landowners, eager to get their lands worked, and blacks, eager to get away from the slavelike gang labor system and achieve something approaching the independence of the small farmer. Blacks worked specified plots of land, earning a portion of the income from them; they moved away from the old slave quarters and, they expected, the watchful eye of the planter.

But if blacks expected that tenancy and sharecropping would put management decisions in their hands, the landlords—at least some of them—expected to provide that management. The resulting conflict concerned the familiar problems of labor-management relations in a free labor, capitalist economy: rates of pay, hours of work, degree of supervision. The particular conditions in the South posed in addition questions of the mix of crops to be grown; the disposition of the crops after harvest; the tenure arrangements on the land; the source, amount, and cost of credit; and, usually, living conditions as well, because housing, rights of fishing and hunting, use of land for gardens and livestock grazing, and rights to woodlots for fuel were a part of agreements between landowners and workers.

How these problems would be solved—or to use more specific terms, what the outcome of the class struggle would be—would depend upon the relative strength of the contending forces.[35] The rapid decline in the activities of the Freedmen's Bureau and the demise of the radical governments ended the minimal protection that such agencies had afforded blacks. The increased power of the planters in the legislatures and the courts provided additional opportunities to solve the labor question. With civil government in their hands and with the black vote controlled by intimidation and fraud, the landlords had the law and the police to secure their interests; and they had little fear of punishment should it be necessary to use extralegal means to control their labor force.[36]

Gradually, the new free labor system had taken shape. Put succinctly, what finally emerged in the southern countryside was capitalistic agriculture. To be sure, capitalism in the South differed from that in the North in a number of important ways that cannot be ignored, but in its basic class structure and its organization of production, it resembled the North more than it differed. Furthermore, in its evolution over time, southern capitalism paralleled that of the North, exhibiting in some areas the same features of concentration and centralization of production.

At the heart of the change in the countryside was the reemergence of the plantation. Not until 1910 did the census bureau recognize what had happened. Since 1870 the census had considered all farming units, whether operated by an owner or a tenant, as separate farms; when it realized that this was misleading, the bureau collected data on "plantations in the South," which were published as a chapter in the 1910 census[37] and then separately in an expanded version in 1916.[38] At about the same time, agencies in the United States Department of Agriculture were compiling information concerning farm management in the South,[39] as were various state departments of agriculture and extension stations.

From this information it is possible to see that the organization of agricultural production took three very different forms. No clear line separated one form from another, and at any given moment an area might be in the process of change and therefore impossible to classify with precision. Nevertheless, by the end of the nineteenth century, the three forms were clearly apparent.

In some places, notably the Delta region and some of the old black-belt areas, there arose large-scale, centrally organized production units that may be best termed "new business plantations." Resident managers and supervisory personnel made all production decisions, owned the land and all tools of production, and owned and controlled the entire output. The work force, primarily black sharecroppers, in practice and in law were considered wage workers who received as pay the value of a portion of what they produced on a parcel of land assigned to them.

A second form of organization was the tenant plantation. Although often large, it was not a centralized production unit. Absentee landlords only casually and intermittently supervised tenants, who paid their rent in money, a proportion of the crop, or a set amount of the crop. Each tenant family worked its individual plot, made its own production decisions, and owned and controlled the output, all subject to liens required by landlords and merchants to guarantee the payment of rent and any loans of money or supplies needed to produce the crop. Both blacks and whites were tenants, the blacks predominating in the old black belt, the whites in the upland regions.

The third form of organization was that of the small landowners. Although they owned their own land, these producers, like the tenants, had to provide liens in order to secure necessary advances. In addition, many mortgaged their land, which meant that when times were bad, they lost their property and fell into the ranks of tenants. Some small landowners were black but most were white, the descendants of the antebellum yeomen farmers.

By recognizing these general trends we can resolve a number of contradictions that have vexed historians. Evidence concerning such matters as the degree of supervision of workers, the power and influence of merchants, and the effects of the lien laws appears contradictory only when the controlling assumption is that of a static agricultural economy displaying minor variations over time and place and by race and class. Once this static view is replaced by what I suggest is a more realistic dynamic picture, apparent contradictions or random variations can be seen as the different characteristics of different systems of production.

Such an approach also provides fresh insights into reformist movements and race relations. Both tenants and small landowners rallied to the farmers' alliances and other farm protest organizations because they faced similar problems. Both suffered from the high costs imposed by their furnishing merchants and from their inability—because of due debts and the lien system—to hold their crops for the best price. Their efforts to build buying and selling cooperatives and to get government aid in the form of cheaper credit and marketing facilities were efforts to solve their economic problems and to establish a degree of economic independence on the land by keeping their costs down and raising their returns.

Sharecroppers, the majority of whom were black, had different problems and different needs. As wage workers they did not control the product of their work; they merely had a claim on a portion of the proceeds of that product. They were paid off as soon as they delivered the cotton to the gin; holding cotton in hopes of a price rise would benefit their employers, not them. Their employers made all the production decisions, and the croppers usually did not deal with furnishing merchants but with the plantation commissary. For most croppers the lien laws were irrelevant. They gave no lien to the landlord because croppers were not renters, and they could give no crop lien because they had no rights in the crop itself. Moreover, because some small landholders and tenants used croppers on their lands, the differences in the needs of the two groups became even more stark. As the merchants squeezed their customers, these customers squeezed their croppers.

Thus, class differences often paralleled race differences. This helps to explain why the alliances could not achieve lasting interracial cooperation. The significance of racism does not disappear in this explanation, but racism can be seen as far more than a completely irrational blindness that prevented unity in the best interests of both groups.[40] The two groups had significant economic and class differences as well.

To insist, as I have, that the Civil War and emancipation brought a revolutionary change to the South is not to insist that the new South shed all the baggage of the past in creating a free labor system. My point is that if we fail to recognize the fundamental change and its effects, we cannot fully understand the nature of the society and the economy of the post-emancipation South. The new business elite that emerged in the postwar South dominated a stunted, static capitalism which, if it made some fortunes, made more poverty by choking off opportunities and stifling economic development. Workers and tenants learned to obey, but they did not learn the responsibilities of entrepreneurship, and they lacked the ability to organize and win political allies to improve their situation. Indeed, their experiences systematically stifled such qualities and in the process destroyed even hopes and dreams. Franklin D. Roosevelt was certainly correct when, in 1938, he called the South "the nation's No. 1 economic problem." That problem was the unfortunate legacy of the massive changes following the Civil War.

Notes

1. The literature on Reconstruction is enormous. Varying points of view among historians may be seen in the following general surveys: E. Merton Coulter, *The South during Reconstruction, 1865–1877* (Baton Rouge: Louisiana State Univ. Press, 1947); John Hope Franklin, *Reconstruction after the Civil War* (Chicago: Univ. of Chicago Press, 1961); Kenneth M. Stampp, *The Era of Reconstruction, 1867–1877* (New York: Knopf, 1965); Rembert W. Patrick, *The Reconstruction of the Nation* (New York: Oxford Univ. Press, 1967); James G. Randall and David Donald, *The Civil War and Reconstruction* (2d ed., rev.; Lexington, Mass.: Heath, 1969); Page Smith, *Trial by Fire* (New York: McGraw-Hill, 1982); James J. McPherson, *Ordeal by Fire: The Civil War and Reconstruction* (New York: Knopf, 1982).

2. W. E. B. Du Bois, "Reconstruction and Its Benefits," *American Historical Review* 15 (July, 1910): 781–99.

3. Among the historiographical surveys that describe and attempt to explain the changing views are Bernard A. Weisberger, "The Dark and Bloody Ground of Reconstruction Historiography," *Journal of Southern History* 25 (Nov., 1959): 427–47; Richard O. Curry, "The Civil War and Reconstruction, 1861–1877: A Critical Overview of Recent Trends and Interpretations," *Civil War History* 20 (Sept., 1974): 215–28; Eric Foner, "Reconstruction Revisited," *Reviews in American History* 10 (Dec., 1982): 82–100. Extensive annotated bibliographies may be found in Randall and Donald, *Civil War and Reconstruction*; and McPherson, *Ordeal by Fire*.

4. Of course, economic and social developments are not completely ignored, but these developments are subordinated to politics. Thus, James McPherson devotes but a single twenty-page chapter to "Social and Economic Reconstruction" in his survey of the Civil War and Reconstruction (*Ordeal by Fire*), which runs to over six hundred pages and more than thirty chapters. A final ten-page chapter "departs from the traditional practice of ending Reconstruction in 1877, and shows how the issues growing out of the war remained vital until the 1890's"; the issues discussed are largely political.

5. See E. P. Thompson, *The Making of the English Working Class* (New York: Pantheon, 1964); Herbert G. Gutman, *Work, Culture, and Society in Industrializing America* (New York: Knopf, 1976).

6. Charles B. Dew, "Critical Essay on Recent works," in C. Vann Woodward, *Origins of the New South, 1877–1913* (Baton Rouge: Louisiana State Univ. Press, 1971), 591. Dew's essay of 112 pages was added to a new edition of Woodward's book, which was first published in 1951. The emphasis on politics is clearly evident in Dew's bibliography.

7.   See Jonathan M. Wiener, "Class Structure and Economic Development in the American South, 1865–1955," *American Historical Review* 84 (Oct., 1979): 970–92, the "Comment" by Robert Higgs (993–97), and Wiener's "Reply" (1002–1006).

8.   See Jay R. Mandle, *The Roots of Black Poverty* (Durham, N.C.: Duke Univ. Press, 1978); Jonathan M. Wiener, *Social Origins of the New South: Alabama, 1860–1885* (Baton Rouge: Louisiana State Univ. Press, 1978); Roger L. Ransom and Richard Sutch, *One Kind of Freedom: The Economic Consequences of Emancipation* (Cambridge: Cambridge Univ. Press, 1977).

9.   See Robert Higgs, *Competition and Coercion: Blacks in the American Economy, 1865–1914* (Cambridge: Cambridge Univ. Press, 1977); Joseph D. Reid, Jr., "Sharecropping as an Understandable Market Response: The Post-Bellum South," *Journal of Economic History* 33 (March, 1973): 106–30, and "Sharecropping and Agricultural Uncertainty," *Economic Development and Cultural Change* 24 (April, 1976): 549–76; Stephen J. DeCanio, *Agriculture in the Postbellum South: The Economics of Production and Supply* (Cambridge, Mass.: MIT Press, 1974).

10.   Recent efforts to deal with some of the issue are the essays in Walter J. Fraser, Jr., and Winfred B. Moore, Jr., *From the Old South to the New: Essays on the Transitional South* (Westport, Conn.: Greenwood Press, 1981). Especially relevant for the point being made here is Dan Carter's historiographic essay, "From the Old South to the New: Another Look at the Theme of Change and Continuity," 23–32.

11.   I am aware that formulating the matter in this way flatly contradicts the work of scholars who have concluded that the antebellum economy was a capitalist economy, and therefore I seem to be accepting merely by assumption the view most clearly associated with the work of Eugene D. Genovese that the antebellum South was noncapitalist or precapitalist. Although I find Genovese's arguments on this question convincing, and they do inform my argument in this essay, I do not think it necessary to enter the debate directly. I am not deducing my argument merely by assuming Genovese's. However, if the South was as thoroughly capitalist both in its institutions and its ideology as is argued by Robert W. Fogel and Stanley L. Engerman (*Time on the Cross*, 2 vols. [Boston: Little, Brown, 1974]), then the problems I describe in what follows would not have arisen. In this sense, therefore, this essay is an indirect contribution to the debate on the nature of the slave society. For Genovese's arguments, see *The Political Economy of Slavery: Studies in the Economy and Society of the Slave South* (New York: Pantheon, 1965); *The World the Slaveowners Made: Two Essays in Interpretation* (New York: Pantheon, 1969); *Roll, Jordan, Roll: The World the Slaves Made* (New York: Pantheon, 1974). See also Elizabeth Fox-Genovese and Eugene D. Genovese, *Fruits of Merchant Capital: Slavery and Bourgeois Property in the Rise and Expansion of Capitalism* (New York: Oxford Univ. Press, 1983), chs. 5 and 6, for a discussion of *Time on the Cross* and its critics.

12.   See, for example, the testimony of workers, union officials, doctors, clergymen, economists, and others before the Senate committee investigating relations between capital and labor in 1883 (U.S. Congress, Senate, *Report of the Committee of the Senate upon the Relations Between Labor and Capital*, 4 vols. [Washington, D.C.: Government Printing Office, 1885], passim).

13.   Horace Mann Bond, "Social and Economic Forces in Alabama Reconstruction," *Journal of Negro History* 33 (July, 1938): 300–301.

14.   Important recent discussions are Eric Foner, *Free Soil, Free Labor, Free Men: Ideology and the Republican Party before the Civil War* (New York: Oxford Univ. Press, 1970); David Montgomery, *Beyond Equality: Labor and the Radical Republicans, 1862–1872* (New York: Knopf, 1967); Daniel T. Rodgers, *The Work Ethic in Industrial America, 1850–1920* (Chicago: Univ. of Chicago Press, 1978).

15.   Montgomery, *Beyond Equality*, 14.

16.   Rodgers, *Work Ethic*, 32.

17.   *Congressional Globe*, 38th Cong., 1st sess., 1188, as quoted in Christie Farnham Pope, "Southern Homesteads for Negroes," *Agricultural History* 44 (April, 1970): 211.

18.   "Work," in the *Fifth Reader* as reprinted in Stanley W. Lindberg, ed., *The Annotated McGuffey* (New York: Van Nostrand, 1976), 270.

19.   This point is spelled out in fascinating detail in Rodgers, *The Work Ethic*.

20.   Edward Atkinson, "The Future Supply of Cotton," *North American Review* 98 (April, 1864): 485.

21.   Ibid., 488–89.

22.   Ibid. 495–96.

23.   Thomas C. Holt, "'An Empire over the Mind': Emancipation, Race, and Ideology in the British West Indies and the American South," in J. Morgan Kousser and James M. McPherson, eds., *Region, Race, and Reconstruction: Essays in Honor of C. Vann Woodward* (New York: Oxford Univ. Press, 1982), 288.

24.   Edward Philbrick to William C. Gannett, Boston, Nov. 21, 1865, in Elizabeth Ware Pearson, ed., *Letters from Port Royal Written at the Time of the Civil War* (Boston: W. B. Clarke, 1906), 317.

25.   *Reports of Assistant Commissioners of the Freedmen's Bureau* (Dec. 21, 1866), U.S. Congress, Senate, 39th Cong., 2d sess., S. Exec. Doc. 6 (Washington, D.C.: Government Printing Office, 1867). The quotations are on pp. 100 and 125.

26.   Capt. Charles C. Soule to Maj. Gen. O. O. Howard, June 12, 1865, "To the Freed People of Orangeburg District" (enclosed in letter), Records of the Commissioner, Letters Received, Bureau of Refugees, Freedmen, and Abandoned Lands [BRFAL], Record Group (RG) 105, National Archives (NA).

27.   Howard to Soule, June 21, 1865, ibid.

28.   For examples, see letters from William C. Gannett, Jan. 26 and March 1, 1863, in Pearson, *Letters from Port Royal*, 147–49, 165–67.

29.   James L. Roark, *Masters without Slaves: Southern Planters in the Civil War and Reconstruction* (New York: Norton, 1977); Willie Lee Rose, "Masters without Slaves," in *Slavery and Freedom* (New York: Oxford Univ. Press, 1982), 73–89.

30.   The best sources for following the conflicts described here (and others as well) are the Annual Reports of the Assistant Commissioners sent to General Howard. These are in Bureau Records, Office of the Commissioner, Annual Reports, 1866–68, BRFAL, RG 105, NA. Useful also are General Howard's annual reports. These have been printed as H.R. Exec. Docs. as follows: 1865, 39th Cong., 1st sess., doc. 11; 1866, 39th Cong., 2d sess., doc. 1; 1867, 40th Cong., 2d sess., doc. 1; 1868, 40th Cong., 3d sess., doc. 1; 1869, 41st Cong., 2d sess., doc. 1, pt. 2; 1870, 41st Cong., 3d sess., doc. 1, pt. 2; 1871, 42nd Cong., 2d sess., doc. 1, pt. 2.

31.   Edwin De Leon, "Ruin and Reconstruction in the Southern States: A Record of Two Tours in 1868 and 1873," *Southern Magazine* 14: (Jan., March, May, June, 1874): 17–41, 287–309, 453–82, 561–90. The quoted words are on pp. 588 and 306.

32.   See Dwight B. Billings, Jr., *Planters and the Making of a "New South"* (Chapel Hill: Univ. of North Carolina Press, 1979); A. Jane Townes, "The Effect of Emancipation on Large Landholdings, Nelson and Goochland Counties, Virginia," *Journal of Southern History* 45 (Aug., 1979): 403–12; Lee W. Formwalt, "Antebellum Planter Persistence: Southwest Georgia—A Case Study," *Plantation Society* 1 (Oct., 1981): 410–29; Jonathan M. Wiener, "Planter Persistence and Social Change, Alabama, 1850–1870," *Journal of*

Interdisciplinary History 7 (Autumn, 1976): 235–60; Gail W. O'Brien, "Power and Influence in Mecklenburg County, 1850–1880," *North Carolina Historical Review* 54 (Spring, 1977): 120–44; Randolph B. Campbell, "Population Persistence and Social Change in Nineteenth-Century Texas: Harrison County, 1850–1880," *Journal of Southern History* 48 (May, 1982): 185–205; James Tice Moore, "Redeemers Reconsidered: Change and Continuity in the Democratic South, 1870–1900," *Journal of Southern History* 44 (Aug., 1978): 357–78; Kenneth S. Greenberg, "The Civil War and the Redistribution of Land: Adams County, Mississippi, 1860–1870," *Agricultural History* 52 (April, 1978): 292–307.

33.   I have discussed this briefly in *King Cotton and His Retainers* (Lexington: Univ. Press of Kentucky, 1968), 303–14, 319–33.

34.   I have discussed the legal changes and some of their effects in "Post-Civil War Southern Agriculture and the Law," *Agricultural History* 53 (Jan., 1979): 319–37; and "Postbellum Social Change and Its Effects on Marketing the South's Cotton Crop," *Agricultural History* 56 (Jan., 1982): 215–30.

35.   This matter has been narrowed by the cliometricians to such questions as the relative profitability of various tenure systems and the most advantageous (i.e., profitable) corn-cotton mix. Some of their critics have dismissed their efforts as being a "market" rather than a "class" approach. Thus far, the effort has kept computers and tempers warm, but the light level has been low. This is unfortunate because the two groups have much to learn from one another. As Gavin Wright has recently suggested, "'class' and market' should not be viewed as incompatible opposites." Wright's brief pursuit of this sensible proposition leads him to important insights; see "The Strange Career of the New Southern Economic History," *Reviews in American History* 10 (Dec., 1982): 164–80.

36.   See Eric Foner, "Reconstruction and the Crisis of Free Labor," in *Politics and Ideology in the Age of the Civil War* (New York: Oxford Univ. Press, 1980), 97–127; Vernon Burton, "Race and Reconstruction: Edgefield County, South Carolina," *Journal of Social History* 12 (Fall, 1978): 31–56; Pete Daniel, "The Metamorphosis of Slavery, 1865–1900," *Journal of American History* 66 (June, 1979): 88–99; William Cohen, "Negro Involuntary Servitude in the South, 1865–1940: A Preliminary Analysis," *Journal of Southern History* 43 (Feb., 1976): 31–60; Carol K. Rothrock Bleser, *The Promised Land: The History of the South Carolina Land Commission, 1869–1890* (Columbia: Univ. of South Carolina Press, 1969).

37.   U.S. Department of Commerce, Bureau of the Census, *Thirteenth Census of the United States, 1910*, vol. 5 (Washington, D.C.: Government Printing Office), ch. 12, 877–89.

38.   U.S. Department of Commerce, Bureau of the Census, *Plantation Farming in the United States* (Washington, D.C.: Government Printing Office, 1916).

39.   See Records of the Bureau of Agricultural Economics, Division of Farm Management and Costs, Reports, Speeches, and Articles Relating to Farm Management, RG 83, NA.

40.   Indispensable on this matter is Barbara J. Fields, "Ideology and Race in American History," in *Region, Race, and Reconstruction*, ed. Kousser and McPherson, 143–77.